Wake Me Up For The Elephants

Comic tales of a restless traveller

By MARJORY McGINN

Pelagos Press

Wake Me Up For The Elephants
Published by Pelagos Press, 2023.
Text © Marjory McGinn, 2023.
ISBN: 9781999995768

Front cover illustration by Anthony Hannaford
(www.anthonyhannaford.co.uk)

Editing and book design by Jim Bruce
(www.ebooklover.co.uk)

All photos, apart from the picture of Brodie Castle,
are the copyright of the author, Marjory McGinn.

About the author

Marjory McGinn is a Scottish-born author and journalist brought up in Australia, now based in England. Her journalism has appeared in leading newspapers and magazines in the UK and Australia. As a feature writer she interviewed many prominent people in the arts, politics and sport, including Donald Sutherland, Olivia Newton-John, Clive James, and cricketing legend, the late Shane Warne, who famously demonstrated his spin bowling techniques for her in a Sydney restaurant using bread rolls!

In 1999, she moved back to Scotland, then in 2010 she set off for a Greek 'odyssey' with her husband Jim and their terrier Wallace, which lasted for four years. The trip became the basis for her four travel memoirs in the Peloponnese Series and two novels, *A Saint For The Summer* and *How Greek Is Your Love?*

For details of the books, author interviews and a link to her blog, visit: www.bigfatgreekodyssey.com

Other books by Marjory McGinn

Dedication

To my late parents, John and Mary McGinn, whose adventurous spirit against the odds inspired my own wanderlust.

"We shall not cease from exploration
And the end of all our exploring
Will be to arrive where we started
And know the place for the first time"

– T. S. Eliot

Author's note

While the stories in this collection are based on factual journeys and feature real people, I have changed the names of many to protect their privacy. I have sometimes conflated parts of the stories or amended them for narrative ease. No elephant, or other wild animal, was manhandled in researching this book. I wish I could say the same for Larry Logue.

Contents

Foreword

The stories in *Wake Me Up For The Elephants* are based on travel trips I made from 1992 to 2006 and include very different locations, but with a common thread. They are comic travel tales laced with candid reflections. The locations featured are among my favourites: Australia, Africa, Fiji, Scotland, Ireland and Greece, where nothing quite goes to plan.

I've travelled a great deal from the age of nine, emigrating with my family from Scotland to Australia as a '10-pound Pom', as British migrants (Pommies) on 'assisted passage' were once cynically described. I'm certain this long ocean voyage ramped up a restlessness for travel and for change.

Later on, as a journalist, many of my journeys were undertaken on media travel trips with small groups of other writers, and mainly while working as a feature writer for a Sydney newspaper. These trips were insightful and often hilarious, taking me well beyond my comfort zone at times: dancing with Pacific natives under the influence of a powerful local brew; dodging a stalker in Mombasa, Kenya; or getting lost on a famously spooky Australian 'rock'. These adventures, and more, are included in this collection.

Some of the latter stories also reflect another life-changing move from Australia back to Scotland in 1999 and touch on the more elusive narrative of seeking to regain a homeland and long-lost roots. This is one of the themes in the chapter *Hysterics in the Heather,* when my mother and I embarked on a holiday in 1995 from Australia to the wilder corners of Scotland, including the Outer Hebrides. It was a comical, transformative jaunt, with a nod to *Thelma and Louise,* involving a car journey, unplanned routes, and occasionally electric bagpipes on the sound system!

This book is also marginally a prequel to my best-selling Greek travel memoir series, starting with *Things Can Only Get Feta*, which was inspired by a four-year odyssey with my journalist husband Jim and our Jack Russell terrier Wallace, from 2010.

I hope the stories in this collection will flesh out in more detail what my itinerant life was sometimes like, even before embarking on the Big Greek Odyssey, which was by no means the end of my adventures.

Cornwall, England, 2023

Chapter 1

Wild women on safari
(Kenya, Africa)

I WAS roused from a deep sleep by a gentle but insistent knocking at the door of my hotel room and a muffled voice telling me: "Ma'am, the elephants have arrived."

I lay for a moment in a bleary state, thinking. *Elephants? What the hell do they want? Maybe I shouldn't have had so much to drink last night.*

"The elephants have arrived!" the voice repeated, louder this time.

Then, of course, I remembered.

"Okay!" I shouted. "Thank you!"

It was only 4am. Despite feeling dead tired and a bit seedy, I grinned with delight.

I've travelled a great deal in my life, particularly as a newspaper journalist, but I've never been woken by room service with the bizarre offer of elephants. But neither had

11

I stayed before at the famous Treetops hotel in Kenya, which was no ordinary establishment.

This was the hotel that in its first incarnation in 1934 had been an eccentric 'safari lodge' in the shape of a treehouse, fixed into a giant mgumu fig tree, on the edge of the Aberdare National Park. Here small groups of select visitors could stay the night and observe wildlife around the vast waterhole out in front, from a safe vantage point. Its most famous guests were Princess Elizabeth and Prince Philip, who were visiting Kenya in 1952 on the first leg of an international tour. It was while the princess was at Treetops she became Queen Elizabeth II on the sudden death of her father, George VI. This event sealed the fate of this remote corner of Kenya for ever.

I crept out of the narrow bed and pulled back the curtains on the barred windows (to prevent animal incursions?) and there they were: three large elephants and a few youngsters cavorting around the edge of the muddy waterhole, enjoying their moment in the hotel's spotlights. It was impressive and worth the wake-up call. There were also rhinos and one stalking leopard. This is what visitors expected from Treetops: to see these creatures living their best lives, not tucked away in a dreary foreign zoo. I sat for a while enjoying the scene and then, tired but happy, slipped back into bed for a few more hours' sleep, with a busy touring schedule starting early in the day.

The previous night, the garrulous, often brash media group I was travelling with from Australia had gathered in the observation lounge after dinner. Through a large window framed by two giant elephant tusks, we watched animals coming and going: zebras, impalas, warthogs ... It was an established custom at Treetops that if you hadn't seen the animals of your choice by the end of the day, you asked one of the receptionists before bedtime to wake you when the animals arrived at the waterhole – no matter what time. My choice was elephants. We'd seen some in the wildlife parks we'd already toured, like the Samburu National Park, but I wanted to see them close up in this iconic and sheltered location.

At the time we were staying in Treetops, in the early 1990s, the hotel had already been enlarged and renovated over the years and was no longer up a fig tree, but it was still unique, with its emphasis on wildlife. No-one would come here for a spa treatment or an hour in the gym, even if they had such things. However, the hotel still carried the spirit of a treehouse: a haphazard-looking building made of wood with thick pylons holding it up. Along the top of the structure was an observation walkway with a sign imploring you: 'Do not feed the baboons. And do not touch them', as if you might even contemplate such a risky venture.

The lounge was the convivial heart of this establishment, fashioned from wood with quirky angles. As its centrepiece, the thick trunk of an old tree growing upwards through the floor and out the ceiling seemed to replicate the feel of a treehouse. A sentimental nod perhaps to the romance of the past.

The group I was with had sat by the observation window for hours the previous night, reluctant to go to bed in case we missed something. We drank quite a few beers, chatting and enjoying yet another unique experience in Kenya that had already yielded so much. The conversations were regularly interrupted by loud exclamations: "Look, guys, the zebras have finally swung by!", or "Check out the face on that hyena down there!" It made a change from the normal flow of social chitchat you find in international hotels.

As journalists, however, it was hard to avoid the Royal history behind the place, and although the original Treetops shack had long gone there were a few reminders of that 1952 Royal visit, including a framed page of the visitors' book, signed 'Elizabeth and Philip'. It listed the animals the couple had seen, 'Rhinos all night (eight at a time)'. They had also seen baboons, warthogs and leopards prowling after dark. What might they have asked to be woken up for? I wondered.

The Royal connection at Treetops may have lost its relevance now, but in the 1990s it still informed the stay, and with stories about Kenya to write up, the group tried valiantly to rope the staff into sharing some juicy anecdotes of the Royal visit.

"Come on, you must know a few good yarns," one of the group, Charlene, asked a waiter in a mock-cajoling fashion. Charlene was a news reporter from Brisbane, a tall, rangy Aussie with spiky blonde hair and a no-nonsense approach that you imagined brooked no opposition from interviewees.

Jason, the PR from the Sydney travel company hosting the trip, lugged into us pressuring staff. "Oh, give the guys a break," he said. "Forget the Royals for a minute. To my mind the most interesting person was the ex-British army officer, Eric Sherbrooke Walker, who built the nearby Outspan hotel in 1927 but wanted to offer guests an edgy wildlife experience as well. So he dreamt up this place. He was one of those eccentric Brits drawn to the shenanigans of colonial east Africa. Shot down in the First World War, he escaped from a prison camp, got himself involved in various scams during Prohibition in America and later came to Kenya. And here's my favourite bit – he didn't invite any journalists here because, as he put it, the smell of the press pack would be upsetting for the wildlife."

He chortled loudly, thinking it rather funny. And I guess it was. Even today, a press pack, to ordinary punters, can often look and smell like a feral collection of humanity. On this particular trip we were to come across one of the more dissolute sons of the profession.

"You're making that up, Jason," said Charlene, dragging on a cigarette, narrowing her eyes at him.

"No, I'm not. It's all on record," he said with a self-satisfied smirk.

Jason was a middle-aged Aussie, laconic, practical. He liked a beer, a barbecue, cricket, a noisy, boysy city bar. He was swarthy, with a low hairline and a derogatory sense of humour, and clearly he had mixed feelings about the media. He'd brought many journalists to Kenya but what he wouldn't have liked about us was that we were, curiously, a women-only group — and forthright ones at that. And perhaps female writers were the only ones who'd responded to his media invitations this time around.

So here we were, five female scribes alone in Africa with Jason. It was obvious he preferred male company, which probably accounted for a certain froideur towards us. During the day he stuck to the usual script, escorting us around the country in a white safari van with our Kenyan driver Darweshi (meaning devout), who some of the group preferred to call Dar because of the Aussie tendency to shorten every possible name. He was a genial guy, with a horde of his own stories about growing up here.

At every hotel during the tour, Jason would retire to the bar after dinner in the hope of finding a like-minded male traveller to drink and blether with, leaving us to our own devices. I admit we were a disparate group of women. Apart from Charlene, there was Sasha, a Sydney freelancer, who wrote for obscure travel publications, although her real obsession was fitness. She was the kind of fanatic for whom a day without sight of a bench press drained the life force out of her, or so I imagined. She did have a set of rock-hard glutes you wouldn't want to tangle with, and a taste for jogging early around every hotel perimeter at first light. Every morning, when Jason discovered her latest exploits, there had been a scene over breakfast.

Agnes was a plain, stocky woman, with long dark hair that she generally wore up in a tight bun. Her best feature was her eyes. When she was surprised by something, which was quite a lot, she resembled a kind of Senegal bush baby, the small marsupial with alert, round peepers. She was 42, she'd informed us, and a magazine journalist of indeterminate subjects but without a travel story to her name, as far as I could tell.

She was one of the most curious women I'd ever met, somewhat old-fashioned, and out of touch with everything to do with the modern world, as if someone had time-travelled her from a Jane Austen novel (a maiden aunt to a sultry heroine, perhaps) and now she didn't know how to get back. All day long we heard her repeated mantra: "Goodness, I don't think I've ever done that before/seen that before/heard that before!" And so forth. However, to her credit, she never baulked at a new experience. Why would she, when the 1990s were fresh to her eyes? She had a lot of catching up to do.

June was a reporter on *The Sydney Morning Herald*, the sister paper to the Sunday publication I worked for. She was the most companionable and well-adjusted of this strange crew, a tall, slim woman with shiny brown hair cut in a bob and in her late thirties, as were the other women, whereas Jason was close to 50. I was pleased she'd come on the trip.

In the observation lounge that first night, Jason had started nattering with a journalist from another media group which had shared the long communal dinner table. He was a lanky, tanned guy with a lascivious glint in his dark eyes and too many laughter lines for his age — which I guessed to be around 35 — as if he'd found life a lot funnier than it really was. He was wearing wrinkled cargo pants and a loud T-shirt with several badges pinned to it. I watched the two men chatting and guffawing, though the younger guy seemed to pay more attention to our female gathering.

He left the lounge early, saying he had a busy day tomorrow, and Jason parked himself briefly next to me, with a drink in his hand. He spoke conspiratorially, leaning his head towards mine, talking with beery breath.

"Nice young journo from Sydney. Larry Logue. Here for another day as well. Sad the other group hooked him or he'd have been on this tour," he said with a sly wink, the meaning of which I didn't quite get, but I could imagine the promise of a male drinking buddy every night would have suited him perfectly.

"Have you come across him? Works for a Sydney daily," he asked.

"Afraid not. Which daily?"

"Now there's a thing – I don't think he said."

"Don't recognise his name at all, unless he writes a motoring column or something else I've never read," I said, crisply.

"I noticed his gaze was fixed on you a lot of the night," said Jason, nudging my arm lightly.

"So ... you're matchmaking in between escorting women around Kenya," I said with light sarcasm, instead of the put-down I'd like to have fashioned, because it's not wise to get too offside with someone who might save you one day from a lion attack.

He smirked. "Well, I gather you're unattached at present."

"No comment," I replied.

Even though we were on this fabulous trip at his behest, as it were, I had failed to warm to Jason. Apart from his gruff personality, I had the uneasy feeling he thought Africa was wasted on women. I gave him a long considered look.

"I came to Kenya for the animals, Jason, not the men," I said, softening the comment with a smile.

He laughed loudly. The other women's eyes swivelled towards us with interest.

"Good for you," he said, slugging his beer and staring blankly through the observation window, as if the answer to life's mysteries lay in the depths of the waterhole — or perhaps he'd seen the slow stalk of the evening leopard.

"Anyway. I'm turning in too. We've got another tour tomorrow and a visit to a native settlement with local crafts for sale. You girls will love that, all those baskets and beads. But don't spend all day about it, right?" Jason said, as he got up and ambled off to his room.

Charlene had lugged into the tone of my chat with Jason and slid onto the bench beside me.

"So, what was Jase going on about?"

"Oh, nothing. Just about the trip tomorrow and other stuff that doesn't warrant a comment. You know what he's like, with us, anyway."

She nodded, funnelling cigarette smoke from the corner of her mouth. "I think Jase would rather be trailing about Kenya with warthogs than women, but that means we're safe from his unwanted attention, hopefully."

I laughed at her Aussie take on things, but little did we know Jason wasn't all we had to worry about.

At breakfast the next morning, Jason was indulging in his usual interrogation of Sasha at the communal table.

"I hope you weren't jogging this morning, Sasha," he said, looking up from his omelette and toast.

"Yep, but not far away," she replied.

"NOT FAR!" he yelped, shaking his head. "Do I have to remind you all that on Kenyan trips we're mostly staying near national parks, with lions, cheetah and God knows what else around these compounds! They won't knock back a bit of prime sheila jogging by. And you won't even hear them coming."

"I wouldn't anyway, Jason. I always listen to music through my ear phones while I run," Sasha countered.

"Oh, Jeez!" he said loudly, rolling his eyes at the rest of us in disbelief. "See guys, this is the attitude that will get you killed, remember that."

"Chill, Jase," said Charlene. "This is Kenya, not Sydney's Botanic Gardens. It's got risks whatever we do. We accept that."

"We don't have to bloody well go in search of them though, do we?"

Charlene shrugged. Agnes laughed. Jason sank into silence, and just when I thought it was safe to enjoy breakfast — the tropical fruits, fresh-baked bread, eggs, bacon, porridge (Agnes went for the porridge, like I knew she would) – Larry turned up. He squeezed onto the end of the long table, across from me. He tried to be attentive, chatty. In the morning light of the dining room he looked mildly handsome, in a young Crocodile Dundee kind of way, without the machete, if you like that kind of thing. But I didn't. And I definitely didn't go for Larry.

After spooning up her porridge, thick with honey and fruit, Agnes started a conversation about what animals we'd all wanted to see the previous night, and if we'd achieved it. I pitched in with the elephants, while the others offered the animal sightings they'd scored.

"What about you?" I asked Larry, just for the hell of it.

"Oh," he said, buttering his toast thickly, devouring half a slice in almost one gulp. "I love all the animals you've mentioned, but I've got a soft spot for those pretty little dik-diks, with the big dreamy eyes, though I didn't see any last night," he said with a wink.

I chortled at the idea of Larry liking dik-diks, unless he fancied catching one and eating it. I'd noticed he had a ferocious appetite at dinner the previous night. And he ate a mountain of food at breakfast, which would account for the fact that although he was fairly tall and thin, he had a curiously rounded stomach, as if he'd just swallowed a koala whole.

"Dik-diks. That's nice. But what are they?" asked Agnes in her usual, otherworldly way.

We had to explain to her they were like tiny antelopes, and I smirked to myself. They were nothing like the slow, sturdy deer she'd have seen around the vast acreage of Jane Austen's country piles, of course.

"I bet Larry'll get in touch with some of you when you all get back to Sydney," Charlene said as we trailed back to our rooms to get ready for the day's safari.

"I hope not," I replied.

"Yeah, I know what you mean. Okay, he's not bad looking really but kind of … you know, creepy."

"I agree."

"He seems keen on you," she said, with a sideways look. "Not just a bit tempted?"

"Oh, no, Charlene, let's not go there, please!"

It's a peculiarity of women that they can sometimes encourage you to go out with someone they definitely wouldn't touch, just for the sake of a date. But then, in Australian cities, there was always a shortage of men, or straight men at any rate, quite the opposite of their bawdy colonial past.

20

The next day our group was heading west, touring the Kenyan sector of the famous Great Rift Valley. Some 3,700 miles long, it carves through Africa from Ethiopia to Mozambique like a deep gash in the earth's surface, formed 40 million years ago by shifting tectonic plates. The Kenyan valley is a fertile region of mountains (including Mt Kenya), indigenous forests and lakes. The discovery of the fossils of ancient humans, around seven million years old, means this part of Africa is often described rather sentimentally as the 'cradle of mankind'.

With its lush gorges and grasslands after the recent October rains, it felt steamy and fecund, like some vast natural laboratory, and proof that more than just humankind had flourished here. At Lake Nakuru we saw one of the world's great bird spectacles: flocks of bright pink flamingos, in their thousands. Darweshi parked the van at the shore so we could take photographs of this teeming mass of wading, chattering birds, so vibrantly coloured that the lake's surface seemed to be on fire, with flames of fuchsia pink.

The following day, we were heading south. I was sorry to be leaving this diverse sector of central Kenya, and especially Treetops. I doubted I'd ever stay in a 'treehouse' again, with a wake-up call for elephants, a circumstance that forever after became an emblem to me of the bizarre and wonderful spin on reality that only adventure travel can bring.

And Treetops in its heyday was one of the most unusual hotels in the world. In the early 1930s, the aim of staying there had been trophy hunting, but by the 1940s the fashion was for game photography, which attracted the Royals. I recalled a story that Charlene had eventually winkled out of one of the staff. He told of how his grandfather had worked at the Outspan hotel in the 1950s and said one of the more remarkable things about the young, 'jovial' Princess Elizabeth was that she was rarely seen without a camera in her hands, or her beloved Cine camera, as she had a penchant for filming animals at all hours. I imagined the Royal archives contained some priceless footage of the early Treetops that no-one would likely ever see, and perhaps a few early attempts at selfies as well, with the couple being photo-bombed on the treehouse terrace by curious giraffes.

The original treehouse was torched in 1954 by Mau-Mau guerrillas, a movement formed a decade earlier by local tribespeople opposed to British colonial rule. It was thought that Treetops had been attacked because of its British and Royal connection. Kenya became a British colony in 1920 but eventually gained independence in 1963, with Jomo Kenyatta as the first President.

After we'd checked out of Treetops, the group assembled at the back of the white safari van, where Darweshi was quietly loading our bags. Jason was impatient to leave. We were heading to the Masai Mara reserve further south for two days before heading back to Nairobi for a night and then flying to Mombasa on the coast. Sasha's bag was first. She was holding it, stepping past Darweshi, trying to load it herself. Darweshi was a methodical man and generally liked to load all the luggage because the space at the back was tight. Somehow Sasha had always got in ahead of him. This time, he was more forceful.

"I'll do that," he said, bending down and taking the bag politely from her hand. His arm dipped slightly and he stood for a moment with a puzzled expression.

"What's the problem, Dar?" asked Jason.

"It's heavy, don't know why. Got some African rocks in there, Sasha?" said Darweshi, with a light laugh.

Sasha was looking away.

"What's in the bag, Sasha? You know we're supposed to be travelling light," said Jason, looking angsty.

"Nothing."

Jason snatched the bag from Darweshi. "Jeeezus …!" Then he dropped it.

"Open it, please, Sasha. I need to know what you've got in there!"

She girned. "Oh, Jase!"

"Don't Jase me. Just do it!"

She bent down and slowly unzipped the soft black bag. Jason elbowed her out of the way and started rummaging through her clothes.

"I don't believe this," he said, pulling out two silver dumbbells and holding them up to show us all. "Four kilos each. Jeez, Sasha! Did you bring them from Oz?"

"Em, no, I bought them cheap in Nairobi. Have to keep up my fitness while I'm away."

Jason looked around the assembled group, his mouth gaping, as if requiring moral back-up, but as usual he was not beyond an indelicate outburst.

"Honestly, guys, what kind of dickhead comes to Africa to play at Jane Fonda in the bush, with lions and wild hippos, while swinging a set of dumbbells?"

Agnes laughed raucously. She'd probably never seen dumbbells before. The rest of us were starting to feel a bit jaded with Sasha's fitness routines. Jason grizzled loudly as he banged the dumbbells into the corner of the van.

"Lose them before the flight to Mombasa, okay, Sasha?"

She gave him a look that curdled an otherwise perfect, sunny morning. That was the moment Larry chose to swing by, whistling one of those indeterminate male tunes, carrying a small packed bag.

He stopped near us and puffed out his chest, as if we might need his assistance.

"Trouble, guys?"

No-one answered. He stood a few moments trying to make eye contact with one of us at least. Nothing. I thought with relief how at least we were parting company with loathsome Larry. He'd soon be far away, no doubt, touring some other far-flung hunting ground with unsuspecting females.

"So, maybe I'll see y'all in Mombasa?" he said in a perky voice, giving Jason some kind of knowing look. But Jason didn't seem to notice. His face was red with rage as he festered over dumbbells.

Surely Larry didn't have the same itinerary? Was he following us? The trip to Mombasa on the coast was supposed to be a relaxing change of pace for a few days before a return to Nairobi on the train. At least Larry couldn't be staying at the same beachside hotel in Mombasa. Or could he? No-one thought to ask.

"Bye, guys. Have a fab day," he trilled, moving off to his own touring van.

Jason was scowling. I'm sure it had dawned on him that this was the first touring failure of his career. He would have made a note to himself: never go on an all-female trip again. Ever! The fact that none of us seemed to fancy him, not even Agnes, must have been a crushing blow as well.

He sat beside Darweshi in the front passenger seat. Although it was supposed to be shared with everyone on a rotational basis because it had the best view, we all noted huffily that he had this position more than anyone else, while we were crammed in the back. He was chatty with Darweshi most days and only drew us into conversation when he saw a new or interesting beast.

"Okay, guys, leopards at two o'clock," he'd say, using the universal co-ordinates for spotting wildlife. "Buffalo at five o'clock.... Giraffes at nine ... Puking lions at three."

We all remembered the day Darweshi had pulled the van to a stop on a scrubby dirt track so we could check out a pride of lions lying under the acacia trees. Half the lions were throwing up, while the others were lying on their backs, looking queasy, moaning. It was oddly comical.

"What's wrong with them?" asked June.

"Eaten a bad piece of meat, I reckon," said Darweshi.

You couldn't help but smile. Lions chundering. It's not what you expect.

"It happens. Something's been out here too long, rotting in the sun. They're hungry, they eat it. Seen it a lot," he said.

The safaris are still what tourists come to Africa for. We'd already had unforgettable experiences, seeing herds of animals moving through some of the many wildlife parks in Kenya: groups of dazzling zebra racing through the scrub; giraffes cantering on their long pipe-cleaner legs; leopards reclining under the acacias, their gimlet eyes on anything passing by. And we'd heard a lot too: elephants trumpeting, monkeys shimmying up trees, screaming blue murder. But mostly we'd heard, even distantly, the sound of animals in their death throes. The one thing that stays with me about our Kenyan wildlife tours was that just about every minute of the day, it seemed, something was being killed, torn to pieces and eaten. It's as normal on the plains of Africa as it is for us to wheel a trolley round the meat counter of a British supermarket, choosing prime cuts. But mercifully we're spared the soundtrack of animals screaming for dear life.

At least in Kenya we didn't see the act itself, only heard it, sensed it, or even smelt it. And danger is always just a breath away. You can't forget for a moment that some of the wild animals you see, or live close to in hotels, as cute as they are, will attack you if they're starving — especially if you jog past them wearing ear phones. A few days earlier we had stayed at a remote hotel built beside a wide muddy river. The rooms were small separate buildings, made of wood, with pointy roofs covered in wooden shingles. A few feet from the riverbank a large sign advised, "Only animals beyond this point", which was comical, like a reminder for literate animals to stick to their own precincts.

In the afternoon of the first day, while being escorted around the compound by the hotel manager and an armed ranger, we saw an alarming sight: a crocodile at the back of the hotel, beside the river, its large head reared up. It was the size of a small motor cruiser. The manager calmed our fears, explaining that a few crocodiles were fed kitchen scraps here every day so they didn't need the extra titbits of humans. Excellent!

However, after the first evening spent in the main building, where we dined, the ranger escorted us in the pitch dark back to our 'huts'. It should have felt safe but in reality it felt like riding a 'ghost train', but with wild hungry beasts behind the moveable props, instead of flimsy phantoms. Things were out there and some were close and suddenly very shouty.

"Baboons," the ranger said, when the animals started up a massive strop in the trees and he saw our fearful looks. "They're noisy, that's all. Don't worry about them."

Oh, but we did later, when they created mayhem above us.

I was sharing a hut with June, and that night as we lay in our simple four-poster beds, from which were draped thin mosquito nets, we heard the baboons screaming in the trees above, swinging between branches, banging their timpani-drum chests. We lay wide awake, listening, unable to sleep.

"What if one lands on the roof here?" I whimpered to June.

"I guess it'll probably crash through it," she replied in a nervy voice.

And there would be no time to speed-dial the ranger. The idea of baboons in the room, and the endless sound of them bitching and leaping above, kept us awake for hours until they finally sloped off. In Kenya there were many nights when most of us slept badly, for one reason or another. There was always something going on: a restive noise, a growl, a shriek, with some creature having the late-night munchies. But therein lies its attraction, too, because the danger can ramp up the excitement.

Darweshi was always mindful of the dangers as we navigated our way through different wildlife parks, including Samburu National Park and the Masai Mara, with its rich cavalcade of animals and the famous migration of wildebeest. He was a delightful character, a native Kenyan, smart and funny, who looked like he could handle almost anything. He had no fear of pulling the van close to lions and lowering the driver's side window a bit to wind them up with pop songs on the radio, fiddling with the volume knob, watching the lions edging closer to the door, teasing them, jokingly, trying to get a roar out of them, which he did. These were among the few times I saw Jason really laugh, enjoying a lads-and-lions kind of moment.

It was Agnes, sitting behind Darweshi, who seemed the most perturbed by the lion antics and wriggled in her seat.

"Don't worry, Agnes," he said. "I know lions. When I was a child I had to walk to school. There were lions about always but it was okay as long as you kept downwind of them." He chuckled softly. I don't know if the story was true or just a tease for us.

Darweshi had the kind of life here we couldn't imagine, although to our western minds it seemed tinged with adventure and the romance of the Kenyan plains. We got a better sense of what his current life was actually like when one day, on our way back to Nairobi, the capital where we were first based, he told us he had to stop by his house to fetch something. I'd imagined him living in a modest apartment in Nairobi, but on the outskirts of the city he stopped the van at a kind of 'settlement' comprised of small shack-like houses. They were set close together but orderly enough and clean-looking. He disappeared into one of the shacks closest to the road.

Charlene leaned towards me in the van, whispering: "Look at where Dar lives. Think about it. Every day he turns up at work immaculate, in a crisp white shirt and neat creases in his trousers." I hadn't noticed the creases until she mentioned them, but she was right. "How does he do that there? And how does he manage to always look so well-adjusted and jovial, when he lives in such modest circumstances?"

I shook my head in answer. The fact he seemed to love his job had a lot to do with it. In terms of what we'd seen in Kenya — slum areas of Nairobi; the small settlements of the brightly dressed Masai and Kikuyu tribes, living some kind of authentic but reduced life on the plains of Africa, but relying heavily on tourist money from selling folk art — Darweshi was probably one of the luckier ones.

He was precise about his job, as we discovered one day on safari when Sasha and I asked if we could have a toilet stop. It earned a rebuke from Jason, of course.

Jason turned to me. "I suppose you're just like Sasha, and have to drink a half litre of water to rehydrate your precious self before you set out from the hotel. No-one else is bursting."

"I am," said Charlene, "but I don't like the look of the hippos."

We were parked next to a waterhole full of hippos, several dozen, with babies too. But the waterhole had a copse of trees close to the van and Darweshi advised us both to head in there for a pee — and be quick about it.

"The hippos can move faster than you think," he said. "They can charge at you when they've got young."

Sasha groaned. Jason sniggered, sadistically.

"Don't worry, Sash. You've got big biceps. You can wrestle a hippo any day," said Jason, having to have the last word as we pulled back the heavy side door and stepped out, hearing it shut loudly and ominously behind us.

"That wasn't funny," Sasha moaned, as we scrambled through the trees, looking for a spot where we were well hidden from the van, if not the hippos. Sasha kept watch while I went first. That was our gambit, but I experienced something I rarely ever had up until then — 'shy bladder syndrome' — and I couldn't pee a drip.

"What's keeping you?" she moaned, holding her stomach and dancing a bit around the scrub.

"Well, Sasha, have you ever peed in front of 30 hippos before?"

She sniggered. "Only when I'm out jogging."

"I'm sure you do, but don't tell Jason. Now let me concentrate."

I have a strange memory to this day of squatting in the undergrowth, festering over snakes and other critters and never taking my eyes off the hippos, the size of Volkswagens. The more I wanted to pee, the more I couldn't, and I had to dither with mind-control, thinking myself somewhere like Africa's Victoria Falls and imagining the deafening roar of water. In the end I managed a pitiful flow, but not before Sasha got tired of waiting and left me to it while she dropped her shorts. Squatting easily with her well-fashioned quadriceps, she completed the manoeuvre in seconds. We legged it back to the van as the hippos started to become restive. Jason was checking his watch as we clambered into the van, but mercifully he refrained from a sarky comment. I felt sure he was chalking up another reason for never taking women to Africa.

* * * * *

After Treetops we drove further south towards the famous Masai Mara Nature Reserve, on the savannah grasslands, which was billed as the high point of this African tour. We hoped to see the phenomenon that travellers still flock to Kenya for: the migration of the wildebeest to Tanzania.

We had two nights in the kind of safari hotel that, although it had a five-star rating, was laid-back and rustic, comprising a compound with tropical gardens, and separate wooden 'huts', which were simple and stylish with ensuites and four-poster beds enclosed by mosquito nets. We arrived there in time for a late lunch and sat in a long open-sided dining room facing the garden. We were in a good mood after a few hours on the outskirts of the Masai Mara, with a longer safari the following day. Even Jason seemed a bit more chipper than usual. We piled into cold meat and crispy salads from the buffet, and great bowls of glistening tropical fruit. All was quiet as we gazed out over the tree-lined grassy garden. The tranquillity was suddenly shattered by an almighty scream.

It was comical, however, the way Jason stopped eating and looked straight along the table for Sasha, as if expecting that she'd just absconded with her dumbbells and was creating havoc with passing wildlife. But she was there, picking away at salad. It wasn't long before we noticed the source of the outburst. A tourist with a small bunch of bananas in her hand had walked towards the trees with the crazy notion of feeding one of the 'cute' monkeys jiving around above.

She waved her bananas teasingly at one of them to coax it down, as if it were a domestic pet. I thought it couldn't end well, and here we were, about to witness pandemonium at three o'clock. The tourist quietly peeled the first banana, waiting for the monkey to jump onto the grass for a feed. But instead, the imp leapt onto her shoulder, snatching the banana, devouring it, while hanging on grimly for the next peeled offering. That's when she started screaming, "Get it off, get it off me!"

Everyone at lunch stopped and stared, clueless about how to deal with a monkey incursion. It was something the guide books never tell you and there were no waiters in sight to help.

The woman flapped her free hand at the monkey, but undaunted, it ripped a second banana from the bunch, still clinging to her shoulder. She took off at that point, running about the garden in wild circles, flapping her arms as if in a tropical fit, and screaming, while the monkey cackled and ate, having the time of its life. Had it not been so unnerving, you might have imagined she was giving a modern dance performance as impromptu lunchtime entertainment.

But help finally arrived when two waiters appeared and sent the monkey packing. After a long silence in the dining room, Jason leaned forwards and glanced around the table, wagging his finger at Sasha.

"You see, Sasha," he said, with a knowing look. "That's what happens when you think you can play fast and loose with wild animals. They bite, they scratch. And God knows what diseases you'd catch if a monkey bit you."

"I don't feed the animals when I'm jogging," said Sasha, with a cocky lift of her chin.

"You don't have to, dear. Give it time and they'll devour *you*. No worries!"

With the mad monkey show over, we silently finished our lunch.

The next morning we returned to the Masai Mara reserve for the day to see the famous migration of the wildebeest, otherwise known as African antelopes, with curved horns and long thin faces, moving in their thousands at this time of year. Darweshi knew exactly where to see the event at a safe distance, under a cluster of elegant acacia trees, but close enough to appreciate the relentless stream of animals (around 1.5 million during the migration, including zebra and impala too), heading to Tanzania, south of Kenya, kicking up dust clouds as they went.

On these spectacular, moody grasslands, it had a biblical effect, as if Moses had just parted the Red Sea and was driving antelopes forward instead of exiles. As it was October, a slightly cooler season with rain, the wildebeest were completing a massive circular route they followed every year, clockwise, from north/central Tanzania, starting in April. They were chasing rainfall and the tender green shoots of the grasslands, up to southern Kenya, through the 15 million acres of virgin savannah that make up the Masai Mara. They then loop round, heading back through the Masai Mara, returning to Tanzania by December, where they calf until March — and start the process all over again.

We sat in the van for over an hour, watching the migration, snapping photos, with no-one bickering, or talking much. It would stay in my mind a long time afterwards: the sheer compulsion of these animals, moving as a group, with their destination firmly programmed in. It was a phenomenon, the likes of which I would never see again.

While the wildebeest soothed our mood for the whole morning, especially Jason's, the afternoon would prickle him again. This time it was my fault. We stopped at a compound where some of the Masai natives lived in a small community in a collection of round wooden huts, their cattle and goats in fenced yards nearby. The Masai are one of the 50 tribes of Kenya and one of the most dominant. Traditionally they have been semi-nomadic pastoralists who have managed to preserve their way of life and traditional diet of raw meat and milk.

At the side of the compound, there was an area set aside with a few stalls selling folk arts, and where the Masai entertained visitors with their famous male jumping dances, called *adamu*. They were all very tall, thin people, both men and women, as if reared to be basketball players. They were graceful and vibrantly dressed in swathes of red material called *shuka* tied at the neck and waist like Roman togas. The women wore beaded hairbands and decorative necklaces comprising many deep rows of coloured beads. The male jumping display, considered to be a show of strength, is famously impressive: quick, impossibly high jumps in succession, as if they had springs in their calf muscles.

"I've never seen anything like *this* before!" said Agnes, with a look of strange amazement. And for once we agreed.

I leaned in towards her and said, teasingly, unable to resist: "What would Jane Austen have made of it all, eh?"

"What?" she said, wheeling round with a look of puzzlement. "What are you talking about? Who's Jane Austen?"

Ah, of course. Agnes in denial now. I smiled to myself. "Never mind," I said as the performance came to an end.

While we eyed up the stalls, with colourful baskets and jewellery, Jason chivvied us along.

"Need to get back to the van, guys, we're a bit behind schedule, and it's getting crowded here." A few more vans had turned up and visitors were milling around.

"We'll only be a minute," said Charlene, abruptly, keen to check out the beaded jewellery.

"No time, girls, no time. Come on, let's get going now!" Jason said, waving his arm at us.

Charlene exhaled loudly with indignation and strode towards the van, the rest of us trailing behind. I too had been keen to look at the jewellery.

When we got back to the van, Darweshi was leaning against it, talking with two of the Masai villagers, as if unaware of Jason's tight schedule. I suspected it was just Jason being typically stressed. We piled inside while Darweshi continued chatting. I noticed a fairly old Masai woman walking towards the van with a woven basket full of beaded jewellery, as if she'd guessed what had been on our minds. I wound down the window and beckoned her over. She held the basket towards the window.

Jason, sitting in front of me, turned and gave me a sour look.

"Ah, when you women are bored, or up against it, there's always beads, isn't there?" he drawled.

"I find that insulting," said June, looking across the aisle at Jason, with a disapproving wrinkle between her fine dark eyebrows.

"Yes, Jason. We all do. It's condescending!" Charlene added, angrily.

It's a bad idea to argue with PRs on media trips, but it's also not a good plan for PRs to insult the people writing up stories that will promote their business.

Jason sighed and backed off for a moment.

"I won't be long," I said, as I pulled out a few items from the basket for a closer look. However, the longer the woman stood there, the twitchier Jason got. He was sighing mightily, as if trying hard to grasp the functionality of decorative beads.

I could sense it was the woman herself who was making Jason twitchy. She was tired-looking, her clothes worn and faded, but it was her teeth that also made me wince. They were in very poor condition and her gums were bleeding, either from the raw meat they traditionally ate, or from some malady or other. She gave me an imploring look.

"Dear God!" moaned Jason, as his eyes flickered towards her. "This isn't a good idea."

Jason could be abrasive, but also squeamish about a lot of things. Did he imagine she had something he might catch? Humility, perhaps?

I agreed it wasn't the best way to shop, out of a van, in a hurry. It was maddening, but I wanted to buy something and chose a deeply beaded necklace and a small bracelet. It was peanuts in our money, so I gave her a bit more. Charlene beside me also wanted to buy something and stretched across to choose a necklace, giving the woman double what she wanted.

"Anyone else want to buy something? If so, speak up now," Jason said impatiently.

Everyone remained silent. I wound up the window and saw the old woman raise her arm in farewell, looking oddly dejected, despite the payment.

Jason turned around in his seat. "Are you happy, girls, with your beads? Though I can't see you wearing them any time soon."

"Shut up, Jase!" snapped Charlene boldly, though he didn't flinch. "Why bring us to these places if we can't see what these people are about, and also buy their folk art and give something back to them. They're dirt poor, as you know, and performing for our benefit."

"Well said, Charlene!" offered Agnes, closer to the front, thumping her hand on her thigh as she said it. Jason turned back towards her, not well pleased, but he said nothing. Too cowed to take on a not-so-otherworldly Agnes right now.

The altercation had drawn Darweshi's attention. In the rear-view mirror, I saw his eyes flicker with interest towards us, and a smile play on his lips, but what he thought of our bickering, I couldn't imagine.

It had been a strange, slightly emotional day on the Masai Mara, watching thousands of wildebeest trailing to infinity, carrying out their destiny with aplomb. But the Masai people were seemingly locked between different imperatives. Less content perhaps with their uncertain destiny, I felt sure, but nevertheless gracious with it.

* * * * *

"Wish I hadn't eaten the zebra in that Animal Bar restaurant," said June, holding her stomach at the airport check-in. "Feel a bit sick."

"Me too," I said, my guts roaring like the north wind.

"Same here," moaned Agnes. "But funny that the meat wasn't striped, was it? That's what I expected."

"Oh, come on, that's a joke, right?" said June vibrantly, even though the notion of Agnes making a joke was improbable.

"No, it's not, June. Didn't you expect stripes?"

"Don't be so absolutely ridiculous! I mean, does leopard meat have spots? Oh, Jeez, save us all!" barked the edgy Jason, turning to the rest of us and tapping a finger on his forehead. It was all so Agnes, and so Jase as well, and it cheered us up in a peculiar fashion.

I was hugely amused, and frustrated at the same time, because the others had failed to understand Agnes's problem like I had. Poor Agnes. Hardly anyone had ever seen a zebra in 18th century England, let alone eaten one.

We had gone to the Animal Bar the previous evening in Nairobi, a few days after we returned from the Masai

Mara. It was a trendy outdoor restaurant, famous in the city, where wealthy locals, international visitors and a few journos went for special occasions or a PR blitz. It wasn't glamorous on international standards but the waiters were good-looking and wore cute waistcoats with faux animal prints, and it seemed a world away from everything else we'd experienced. Platters of food were ferried to our table, with several cuts of animal: zebra, crocodile, buffalo and barramundi fish. No giraffe or lion steaks, mercifully.

"Oh, what would elephant taste like?" Agnes trilled.

"Don't even go there," Jason remarked, gnawing on a crocodile steak.

He knew us fairly well by now for the weaklings and eccentrics we seemed to be and he explained that the creatures we were devouring weren't wild but farmed especially for restaurant consumption. As if that really made it easier. A crocodile is exactly as you expect it to be, like gnawing on an old tyre.

None of us ate very much but despite that we were all queasy the next morning as we waited for our flight to Mombasa. Jason wasn't feeling sick, of course. He'd done all this many times before and he enjoyed telling us that men were superior creatures when it came to holding down food — or peeing alongside hippos.

But it wasn't just food torture Jason had in mind at the Animal Bar. He'd also spotted an 'amusing' PR opportunity and organised a camera crew from a local TV station to be there to interview us after the meal to give our Aussie impressions of Kenya.

We stood in a line under the trees waiting for our turn to gabble about lions and elephants and so forth, flattered and embarrassed at the same time. While I waited for my five minutes of African fame, some cunning beetle or nameless critter landed on the back of my head and started to burrow into my hair, which is curly and nesty at the best of times. It meant that while I was being filmed, I was possibly talking gibberish, or more than usual, and moved my head incessantly to shake out the critter. And because it's better to make mileage out of a media mishap than look foolish, I decided to fess up on camera to the beetle incursion. It caused a pleasing ripple of mirth among the diners and camera crew, especially the extraction bit when the restaurant manager ploughed into the scene. He raked about in my hair and retrieved a critter, holding it up for the camera. It was something big and black, waving menacing pincers, and I was assured the critter was harmless. So why the haste to extract it?

After 10 days touring the unforgettable Kenyan wildlife parks and the Rift Valley, we were flying to Mombasa on the east coast to a five-star beachside hotel with a covered pool terrace, complete with piano bar. It was a place where we began to feel like we were properly on holiday. And much as we had loved them, there were no wild animals in sight. No lions listening to radios, baboons sparring above us, or insolent monkeys.

"This is a nice change, isn't it, girls?" said Jason at the bar, looking more laid-back and conciliatory than we'd seen him of late, twirling the cocktail umbrella in his glass. "Look, I know the safaris were awesome, but also hard work in a way, so you've got a few days here to recharge your batteries, swim, do nothing, go shopping in Mombasa, whatever."

"He's being gracious and sweet all of a sudden," said Charlene, with characteristic cynicism, as we spread out on sunbeds around the pool after lunch. A big guy who looked like Louis Armstrong was on the piano singing *It's a Wonderful World* in a rich velvety voice, with the sea sparkling in the distance.

I couldn't think of a more perfect tableau in this part of Kenya, until I saw a familiar shape through the big French doors leading to a grassy terrace. Larry! He was like a lone leopard at the Treetops waterhole. My stomach did a queasy cha-cha. He was standing with another group of tourists in smart beach outfits, drinking, laughing loudly about something. As usual he was a sartorial disgrace in grubby shorts and walking boots, his koala tummy pushed out in a too-tight, daft kind of tourist T-shirt emblazoned with animals. Of course, it was inevitable he'd turn up here with his tour gang. It was, I now realised, THE place to be on the Mombasa coast.

I got up and plunged into the pool and swam several cooling laps, hoping that one of the pouty blondes hovering near Larry at two o'clock in safari co-ordinates would spirit him away and, if we were really lucky, feed him to some passing great white shark.

* * * * *

"I've never been to a disco before," said Agnes after her second cocktail, licking the handle on the red paper parasol bobbing in her glass.

"What?" said Charlene, giving me a knowing wink. I'd now had time to explain my jokey theory of Agnes and her time-travel misadventures. Charlene had lapped it all up, enjoying the madness of it.

"I definitely think you're right about Agnes," Charlene whispered in my ear when Agnes was distracted by someone on the dance floor. It was Larry, doing ridiculous un-coordinated moves, as if he'd lost control of his knee joints. He was dressed in tight black jeans and a hideous shirt with a Polynesian theme of grass-skirted women, possibly from an earlier travel junket.

The hotel disco that first night, on the open deck at the top of the building, was a cracking weekly feature of the hotel, with a lively DJ in a corner playing the top tunes of the day. We had been dancing and drinking for a few hours already and time had slipped by as easily as a baboon tree-hopping.

We were sitting at a round table catching our breath after the last dance session to Ace of Base. Charlene looked sexy in a tight short dress, wearing lashings of make-up. Agnes was in a wide blue dress of indeterminate origin, nipped in at the waist with a heavy belt. She wore flat, practical shoes. Only a jangle of wooden bracelets bought at a folk-art shop in Nairobi gave any sense that she was out of her normal zone, and enjoying the experience. Her hair was long and loose on this occasion and I detected a smear of red lipstick. These modifications made her look rather striking, in a bizarre way.

"You should wear your hair like that more often," said Charlene. "It suits you."

Agnes blushed, or maybe she was feeling hot and bothered after a short attempt at disco dancing, which seemed not to be her thing. Charlene winked conspiratorially in my direction, as if expecting Agnes might choose tonight to break loose. Ah, not in this century, I felt sure.

Sasha was dressed in a long flowing top and cycle shorts, showing a pair of knotty calf muscles. June looked elegant in a short white dress that had drawn, unknown to her, Larry's sly admiration from afar. We were an even more mismatched-looking group when properly dressed for socialising.

Jason was wearing black trousers and white shirt and looked like a waiter. He was smoking a lot and drinking beer after his cocktails. He seemed slightly bored. When the DJ took a break, Jason summoned Larry over from a table across the dance floor and made room for him, beside me, which was a bit of a squeeze. I felt his sweaty forearm slide against my own. I'd been enjoying the evening until then.

"Jeez, you all scrub up well, girls!" Larry said, casting a slightly bloodshot look around the assembled women. There was something of the opportunistic sleaze about Larry, taking advantage of the fact we were women trapped in a social situation in a hotel in Africa. By the very nature of media trips, and the protocol of always having to behave reasonably in the midst of PRs and hotel owners, we couldn't tell Larry to sling his hook. Well, not yet anyway.

"This is a tame disco, isn't it?" he said, after sculling some of his beer.

Everyone disagreed and only Agnes broke ranks. "I guess it is," she said, from the shallows of her disco expertise.

I smiled to myself, wondering what Agnes's life was really like in Sydney, where she lived, what hobbies she had, or if there was a boyfriend perhaps. I was musing over all this when I heard Larry pipe up.

"Let's go to another disco in town. I've heard there's this place called the Safari Bar. It's the coolest thing in Mombasa."

"A proper African disco. Great idea," said Charlene, a few cocktails too many dulling her good sense and ramping up her adventurous nature. "Sounds different and we'll get some fab copy out of that."

"Or someone else will get the copy, Charl, when you end up dead in a vacant lot somewhere in the small hours," moaned Jason.

"Oh, don't be so ridiculous," said Charlene loudly. "It's Kenya, not Rwanda. Anyway, there's six of us, including Larry." She offered him a cursory glance. He was smiling warmly, enjoying this bit of mischief and discord, I felt sure.

"And there's you, of course, Jason, as our chaperone," said June.

Jason looked horrified. "I'm not going to the Safari Bar with you lot. I know the place, incidentally. It's a slick pick-up joint favoured by local men looking for naïve sheilas like you lot .... unless, of course, that's all you're looking for, girls, eh?"

"We just want a bit of *fun*, that's all, Jason. We've been cooped-up in a van for weeks, staring at wild animals," said Charlene, who added quickly, "Lovely as they are, Jase. But we just need to chill a bit, eh girls?"

"Isn't this all about chilling?" said Jason, waving an arm towards the dance floor.

"Of course, but you know what I mean," Charlene said, blowing air out between her scarlet lips.

Larry, who'd been quietly pushing his beer mat around on the table, suddenly piped up: "It'll be fine, Jase. I'll look after the girls." He winked at June and, at the same time, twitched his leg against mine under the table.

"It's a bad idea, guys, honestly. It's midnight now. The hotel PR is giving us an official tour of the hotel after breakfast tomorrow. I don't want you all turning up after three hours' sleep, hung over, or worse. May I remind you all, you're media guests here and not at some Gold Coast hens' night back in Oz," said Jason.

"Spoil sport!" said Agnes censoriously, which was quite comical. "I for one would love to see a proper Mombasa disco, with locals, and okay, a bit of danger."

My head was spinning, thinking of Agnes going wild in a Mombasa nightclub, out of her depth completely, doing the waltz to *Pump Up The Jam* by the band Technotronic.

"Well, I'm going to turn in," said June. "It's been a long day, and I'm still queasy after the zebra dinner." But I guessed it was Larry's sudden attention that was souring her stomach.

"Me too," I said, feeling similarly queasy.

"I took you for a gamer sheila than that," said Larry, nudging his elbow into my arm unpleasantly. "Look, you'll never get a chance to see a Mombasa disco again."

"Larry, it's not high on my wish list of things to do in Africa."

Larry sneered and toyed again with his beer mat.

Jason sat broodily, his arms crossed over his chest. It seemed his lone male buddy was starting to annoy him as well.

"With respect, Larry, you are not part of our tour group, so you shouldn't be leading these women astray. We have our own agenda, RIGHT!" he snapped, picking up his cigarette packet and lighter, glancing round the table.

"Look, guys, I can't tell you not to go. You're not in a chain gang here. But I will be bloody furious with you all if you turn up for the hotel event tomorrow looking like you've slept in a bear pit all night, which I might remind you the Safari Bar is, really. But if you're determined to go," Jason added, glaring at me, as if he suspected I'd weaken and join the excursion in the end, "I suggest you get the concierge to call you a taxi and ask the driver to come back to pick you all up at a certain time. Or failing that, take a gun with you. Good night!"

He walked away, shaking his head.

Agnes sniggered. "Where does he suppose we'll get a gun?"

"He was joking, Agnes," said June, putting a hand on her arm.

I might actually have been daft enough to go with the women if Larry hadn't been there. But with images whirring in my mind of everything that could possibly go wrong, and the prospect of Larry practising his seduction moves under a flashy disco ball, I thought, Nah! I'd rather drop my knickers at the hippo pond any day.

"Well, what's got into Jason? I thought he was a sociable kind of guy," said Larry in a sulk.

The others ignored Larry's lack of insight and tried to sell June and me the merits of a Mombasa disco. Surprisingly, it was Agnes who was most insistent, and petulant. I should have seen that coming with the change of hairstyle.

"You two are behaving like maiden aunts," she said sniffily, as we got up to leave. We bade them goodnight and walked silently to the lift. When we got inside, we chortled madly at Agnes describing anyone as a maiden aunt.

"How funny," said June. "But you know, I'm sure deep down the girls know the disco's a bad idea, but they just don't want to say so, even Charlene."

I nodded in agreement but I also knew from experience that they didn't want to break with the custom of Aussies on a media junket far from home, going troppo on expenses. We had all done it, to varying degrees. But this seemed an edgier kind of troppo.

"What do you think they'll decide in the end?" asked June.

"God knows."

"Well, I guess if Larry's with them they should be ... sort of okay." She pulled a face.

"Are you kidding? That's like leaving the lions in charge of the dik-diks, isn't it? Larry's favourite beast, remember."

"Oh, yes, he would like the small vulnerable animals best of all."

I slept fitfully that night and when I awoke in the morning, I started to dread a scene at breakfast as the disco queens began to reappear after their night in the bear pit, with Jason girning over the sight of them. But when I got to the dining room, I was surprised to see the girls sitting fresh-faced and neat, apart from Charlene, who looked slightly hung over. Sasha was, as usual, revitalised by an early-morning jog around the compound.

They said they'd changed their minds after all about the disco. No explanation was offered. I noticed, from a quick glance at the other media group at a nearby table, that Larry was missing, having gone apparently to the disco alone in a taxi. He hadn't been seen back at the hotel yet. I can't say I had a shred of alarm about that.

"How are the maiden aunts this morning?" smirked Agnes, looking at her watch, her hair pinned tightly up again. "Later than us, anyway."

"Don't start, Agnes, or any of you," said Jason, glaring dulled-eyed around the table, as if he'd also by some quirk had a long night at the Safari Bar. "Let's all be calm and sensible today, okay."

I laughed. I couldn't help it.

The hotel tour took ages but was convivial enough and sweetened by the offer of champagne and canapés before lunch, after which Jason told us the afternoon was ours to do what we wanted. However, it didn't stop him inquiring what we had in mind exactly, as if he didn't trust us.

Charlene told him we'd decided to tour Mombasa old town and its markets.

"Okay, good idea. But listen up now. I'll organise a hotel vehicle to take you there, which will give you a bit of a tour of the old town, right? I expect you'll want a few hours for your shopping, so it's probably easiest if you just get a taxi back when you're ready. Try to flag down one of the registered black cabs, if you can. They look like London cabs, okay? They're the safest bet. And if you can't find one, call the hotel concierge and, hopefully, he'll organise something for you."

"Just use your common sense," Jason added, glancing at Agnes, then quickly looking away. I think he had the measure of Agnes too now. While she looked prim and sensible, he'd already had that gut feeling that she was 'other', but what kind of 'other' he still wasn't sure, like the rest of us really. Only Sasha wanted to stay at the hotel, to work out in the fitness centre, unremarkably.

Mombasa is the largest port town in east Africa. First settled by Arab traders, and later conquered by the Portuguese in the 6th century, it has a mix of architectural styles. After our tour of the old town and its attractions, which all took longer than we expected, we got the driver to drop us off in the traditional market area, off one of the narrow lanes, where classical houses with peeling facades were hunched against cafes, curio shops and spice and scented-oil emporiums wafting out pungent aromas. The market area was vast, selling food and everything under the sun, with dozens of stalls offering Kenyan folk items, like the colourful *kiondo* bags, woven from native grasses.

Having haggled over a vibrant striped bag with leather trim, I was standing at a stall of beautifully carved wooden animals that were popular with tourists. I was appraising a 3ft-high giraffe when I felt an unnerving presence beside me. Smelt it even, like a smouldering bonfire. Larry. My eyes darted briefly towards the same black trousers and Polynesian shirt he'd worn the night before.

"Did you come here straight from the Safari Bar?" I asked, addressing my question to the giraffe.

"You don't like me, do you?" he slurred, like a petulant child. I turned and looked at him, noting the dark stubble on his face and that his brown eyes were livid with tiny bloodshot highways.

"At this moment, Larry, not much!" It was too late now to be gracious.

He didn't respond.

"Why are you wandering around the market?" I asked him.

"The Safari Bar's up the road."

"Ah, so no sleep then, by the looks of things."

He shrugged. "I think I slept somewhere but can't remember where."

Oh, I could well imagine.

"I wouldn't buy that giraffe if I were you," he said, pointing a grubby finger towards it. "Years ago an Aussie friend brought a wooden giraffe back from Kenya and after it stood for weeks in his house, creatures started to burrow their way out of it – big horrible bugs."

So, that's how Larry was born. Interesting!

He moved off towards a nearby stall selling wooden bracelets, trying some on, messing up the display. While his back was turned, I gave him the slip and raced through the market until I'd rounded up the girls, loaded up with their purchases.

"Listen up. Larry's just turned up here, looking feral. Spent the whole night in the disco, no doubt. I think we should get back to the hotel. We've been away for ages anyway. We can have some 'me' time around the pool."

"Aw, he really does like you," drawled Charlene, looking hung over again. I guessed she must have stayed at the hotel disco into the early hours.

"Oh, please, give me some credit for having a bit of taste. Larry's a prick. Well, he is today. So, back to the hotel, what do y'all say?"

"Another excitement-avoidance tactic," said Agnes, with a curl of her lip.

"Oh, Agnes, he's all yours if you want him. Go for it. None of us will stop you getting your leg over," I offered, crudely.

June sniggered loudly, which wasn't like her at all. But here's the thing: after nearly two weeks on safari with the grumpy and resentful Jason; staring into an utterly beautiful but wild predatory abyss, complete with full sound effects and more, delicacy seemed a bit redundant.

"Yeah, let's hit the road," said Charlene, brightening suddenly. "I could do with a pool swim and a strawberry daiquiri, or five. And you're right, hon, Larry's a busted flush."

"Okay, so let's schlep away and flag down a taxi."

With Larry seemingly in the midst of the market, still haggling over bracelets, we walked towards a busy road and carefully tracked up the median strip, searching for a black cab coming either way.

"I can't believe there are even black cabs in Kenya," said June.

"Good point," said Charlene as we watched various old makes of clapped-out cars crawl past us.

"Yes, there are proper English black cabs, a relic of colonialism," piped up Agnes, suddenly a font of local knowledge.

But then something else came into view. Not a black car but a heap of a thing, yellow, dinged here and there, with a 'taxi' sign like a witch's hat perched on top. It rumbled to a halt beside the opposite kerb. The driver got out and waved us over.

The girls were keen. "Wait," I said, holding out a protective arm to keep them back, starting to morph into group mother. "Remember, we're supposed to get a black cab." I recalled that Darweshi, too, before we'd left Nairobi, had also warned us to go for a black taxi if we ever needed one, and never, ever to get into anything else. This was 'else'!

The driver kept waving us over. He was a wiry figure sporting big hair held in check by a colourful knitted hat. Not your usual black-cab attire, at any rate. The girls were in a mutual zone, tired, thinking of pools and cocktails, and raced across the road excitedly, weaving in and out of traffic towards the 'taxi', with me sprinting behind. That's when I turned and noticed Larry in the distance, legging it fast up the road towards us, putting an evil spin on this doomed trip. My stomach lurched with anxiety.

"It doesn't look anything like a taxi," I said to the others, as they fingered the door handles, the driver ushering us inside quickly. There was some virtue in that because Larry was gaining on us bit by bit, even though he seemed out of puff, unsurprisingly after his night in the bear pit.

Charlene jumped into the front passenger seat. I sat behind her on the left, June beside me, then Agnes. When we tried to pull the doors shut they seemed shoogly, sagging on their hinges. No sooner were they shut than they wanted to ping open again. My forehead was beading with nervous sweat. This wasn't a good idea. We saw the driver sprint round the car, grab each door, lift it slightly and slam it hard shut, and then lock each door with small slide bolts level with the bottom of the window frames, which we hadn't noticed in our rush to get in. Charlene turned and gave me a twitchy look.

"Well, that's us locked in," I said.

Even Agnes was quiet, wringing her hands lightly. Just as the driver got inside the car, Larry arrived, breathing hard, banging on the roof to get our attention.

"Drive on!" shouted Charlene, but the driver turned and looked towards Larry, unsure of what to do.

"Is he with you?" he asked.

"No," I told him. "Let's get going!"

But Larry had managed to unbolt the door next to Agnes. He pulled it open and pleaded to be let inside. It was quite a wide make of car but there was no way we could fit four along the back seat.

June leaned over Agnes and firmly told him: "Sorry, but no room."

But Larry was having none of it. He wanted to get back to the hotel with us.

"Be reasonable. One of you girls can sit on my lap if you like," he said, his road map eyes scorching in my direction.

"No thanks!" I snapped. But in the end, because we just wanted to get out of the town, we let him in, with me, the smallest of the group, sitting on June's lap and Agnes beside us. Larry sat at the window, and the driver had to get out again to bolt Larry in. The car suddenly filled with the dank odour of cigarettes, alcohol breath and sweat. I felt sick.

When we drove off, the car's engine was coughing and wheezing. To call this vehicle a car was a stretch. This was a rusting death shell with bald tyres. Inside it had a steering wheel and gear shift, but no dashboard to speak of and no dials. It had no proper suspension either, and the seats seemed to have been plundered from other wrecks of cars and dropped in. As we motored slowly up the road, you could feel every pothole and bump. And it was a fair drive back to the hotel.

Kenya wasn't known as a drivers' paradise. Locals apparently had scant regard for road rules, as I'd read in an official government brochure. "Although they do exist, many locals do not follow traffic rules in Kenya," it explained. "That may entice you to consider alternative transportation, such as renting a car with a driver. According to Kenyan laws, the norm is to drive on the left, but locals will drive on the wrong side of the road whenever they encounter a pothole, or an animal in their way."

That would account for why our driver swerved and swore and grazed the median strip every minute or so. I could hear Charlene cursing in the front passenger seat. I feared we'd have an accident and was reminded of the consequences of that in Kenya, when I thought of our serious first-aid kits that were compulsory for each of us to buy from a government health organisation before we left Australia.

They contained, among other medical bits and pieces, two sterile syringes. In the event of one of us ending up in hospital and needing injections, we'd been advised to keep the syringes with us always and offer them to hospital staff because Aids and various tropical diseases were rife in Africa in the 1990s. None of us had bothered to carry the kits on this city tour, of course.

As the driver barrelled on up the road, veering about and squawking at other drivers like a drunken parrot, Agnes piped up: "Goodness, this drive! I've never done anything like this before." But it was offered without her usual naïve demeanour.

"What, you mean like sailing up the Barcoo in a barbed-wire canoe?" Charlene said loudly from the front seat, using an Aussie expression I knew the driver wouldn't get. The Barcoo is a river in the Australian outback redolent with crocodiles.

All the way back to the hotel, I had an increasingly bad feeling about this expedition, locked in a lethal tin can with a sleazy Aussie male and a wily, duff driver. It couldn't end well. As if things weren't bad enough, Agnes thought she'd pass the time by talking and wanted Larry's account of the Safari Bar the previous night, despite the awful disco fug he gave off.

He said he couldn't remember much, only that we wouldn't have liked it. Too hot, too noisy, but from his point of view there were plenty of women, mostly foreigners. The thought of it made me feel sick again. I tried to wind down the window next to me but the handle came away in my hand.

"So, did you pull last night, Larry?" asked Agnes.

I nudged her with my elbow.

"I may have, Agnes, if you're interested."

"No, we're not interested AT ALL!" I said, firmly.

He gave me a black look. "Of course, madam here isn't interested in what I have to say. She once remarked she didn't come to Africa for the men, but for the animals. Very noble. I came for the adventure, and any women I meet along the way, well, they're fair game to me."

He laughed, making an ugly sound like sandpaper on metal. The driver laughed as well, though he couldn't have known what we were talking about. So, two hyenas, with four women to prey on.

"There are easier places to pull than Africa," said Charlene, archly.

"And you would know that because…?" Larry drawled sarcastically.

"Okay, guys, let's pipe down now," said June, showing the calm authority I admired about her. It had a sobering effect for a few moments at least.

But Agnes hadn't quite finished and half turned towards him.

"Larry, have you looked at yourself today? What woman is going to lock thighs with you? Honestly, I'd rather dance with a rotting goanna than take you on!"

There was a heartbeat of silence and then we all burst into gales of laughter and Larry shut up at last, hunching against the grubby side window. Charlene turned and winked at me. I gave Agnes an admiring pat on the hand. She was catching on – sometimes.

I'd had enough though and I devised a plan as soon as the driver told us he needed to stop at a garage for petrol. When he got out, I leaned towards Charlene and whispered: "Can you crawl over to the driver's side and get out, and unlock my door, I need some air. Feel sick."

I looked over at Larry and, fortunately, he had his head back on the seat and seemed to be dozing. Charlene quietly levered herself across the hand-brake and slipped out of the unlocked door. She then unbolted my door and let me out. June and Agnes followed. Agnes was about to talk but I put my finger over my lips to shush her. I gently shut the back passenger door and slid the bolt.

I drew the girls into a circle. "Listen up now. Let's get out of here. I have a bad feeling with all this, and I want to get rid of Larry most of all."

I explained that since he seemed to be asleep, we'd pay the driver something and then make our way back to the hotel, somehow.

"Yeah, let's do that," said Charlene.

The driver was amenable. He didn't care what we did as long as he got a payment for the trip so far. I asked him if, before dropping Larry at the hotel, he could take him on a nice trip around the outskirts of Mombasa because Larry, I said, with a look of faux sincerity, was very keen to see more of the local area. I told him Larry would pay for that leg of the trip himself, no worries.

Larry was still asleep when the driver turned onto the road again, the car sliding about on its tyres like a rookie skater, black smoke belching from the exhaust pipe. We watched from the safety of the garage forecourt. Larry must have woken up then and, realising we'd gone, turned and looked out the back window with that cartoon face you see on children in the back seat of the family car, taken out for a boring Sunday drive with the oldies. We all waved and then his head slumped back wearily against his seat.

"Well, Agnes?" I asked gently when we were finally in the back of a comfortable car sent out by the hotel after we'd made an emergency call. "Was our taxi trip from hell too adventurous even for you do you think?"

She nodded. "You could say that. And you know, there are certain times in life when a bounder finally needs to be put firmly in his place."

Well said, I thought. Jane Austen would have been proud.

* * * * *

The overnight train back to Nairobi was unexpectedly pleasing, with a shabby chic aura and a feeling that not much had changed since the heyday of Kenya's colonial past. Jason chivvied us into the dining car not long after we set off. We sat at two scuffed wooden tables across the aisle from each other. There wasn't much on the menu, apart from lamb curry and some old-fashioned British desserts.

We drank beer and watched the scenery flash past us, the flat-topped acacia trees always to my mind like trees caught in a hurricane and pushed out of shape by the wind. We caught sight of animals too, in the glimmering dusk, that we had hitherto been so close to on safari.

"I've done this train trip a few times now and the food's amazing, honestly," said Jason, seeming to be in a very good mood for once, perhaps from the realisation the trip was ending in a few days and he'd be shot of this gaggle of 'sheilas'.

His enthusiasm for the food didn't quite cut it for us, remembering our queasy dinner of zebra and crocodile in Nairobi. I kept wondering how an African curry would bed down with us for the evening.

This particular train trip had famously been written up in some of the Kenyan guide books I'd read, lauding the sartorial splendour of the waiters in their smart white jackets. Such guidebooks were probably written during the colonial era as well. The jackets today were sadly not so pristine and had an over washed, indeterminate grey look about them, and the waiters looked tired. But they were stoical, running up and down the aisles with practised ease on steady train legs, ferrying great steaming white plates of curry.

Despite any misgivings, the curry was delicious, and the spotted dick with custard (another hangover from colonial days?) wasn't bad either, if filling.

The first-class sleeping cars were perfunctory but clean. I shared a room with Charlene, who had grown in my estimation during the trip. I liked her no-nonsense Aussie approach. We chatted for a while as we got ready for bed. She stood at the small washbasin brushing her teeth, cursing when she realised she had no bottled water left, and a mouth full of toothpaste, which she spat into the sink.

"Have some of my water," I offered.

"Nah, don't worry. I'll just swallow," she said with a wink into the mirror.

"Oh, don't do that!"

"Why not. How bad can it be? I've just eaten a curry on Kenyan railways, and before that the zebra and crocodile in Nairobi, and I never thought I'd ever say something as ridiculous as that – ever."

I laughed heartily. "That's true. How bad can toothpaste be? But let's hope the curry behaves itself and sits well for the rest of the trip. I don't fancy a dash to the toilet during the night."

We lay in our bunk beds, under starchy sheets, me on the bottom, staring across at the window as the grasslands of east Kenya rushed by.

We talked for a while, going over the trip so far, remembering the outstanding moments but having a laugh at the misadventures and the things that journalists are willing to put up with in the name of media junkets: crabbit PRs, wild animals screaming in the night, risky menus, hippos in the 'ladies' toilet', chundering lions, and much more besides. And there had been unexplained queasy, challenging days for everyone, notwithstanding our dinner at the Animal Bar.

Then we touched on Larry and the feral taxi misadventure in Mombasa and laughed like hyenas as the train chugged its way deeper into darkness.

"On a more serious note," I offered. "What do you think happened to Larry after he went off in that taxi?"

She was quiet for a moment. "No idea. Never saw him again at the hotel. Jason never mentioned him again, and none of us seemed inclined to analyse it, did we? Funny that! But Larry must have legged it with his group to some other location and never said goodbye."

"I suppose so. If anything had happened to him on that taxi journey back to the hotel, Jason would have known for sure. Someone would have, wouldn't they?"

"You'd think so, but why do you care? You're not feeling guilty about that greasy goanna," she chortled, remembering Agnes's colourful put-down of Larry as an Aussie lizard.

"No, of course not. He was an appalling guy. Just wondering, that's all."

As I heard Charlene snoring lightly in her bunk above, I constructed some alternative fates for Larry, missing his flight home perhaps and cutting loose in Africa amid its fecund tangle of beauty and danger, stalking new adventures amid its harsh imperatives, amid the hunting and gorging on a daily epic scale. Or perhaps, finally, the bubbling cauldron of human creation that still seemed to roil away within the slopes of the Rift Valley had sucked Larry back into the primordial soup for a mental refit.

At that point, hypnotised by the gentle rock and rattle of the Kenyan train, I fell into a deep sleep, waking at dawn as we moved through the Nairobi National Park.

I crept quietly out of bed and sat by the window a long while as flat acacia trees slipped by and, in the misted spaces between, groups of animals trailed slowly like hungry ghosts. And there were elephants too that I didn't need an organised wake-up call to see. In this epic landscape, their bold dark shapes were backlit by the rising sun. It was a unique snapshot, raw and thrilling, that I would never see in this life again.

* * * * *

After we got back to Sydney, out of sheer curiosity, or perhaps a sliver of guilt, I rang a few contacts on Sydney papers and asked about Larry. No-one had heard of him. And in the weeks after we returned, I never saw a bylined travel piece from him on Africa, which the PR of his own media group would have expected. And Jason never mentioned him either. Not that we saw or heard much of Jason.

After all our travel pieces on Kenya appeared in various publications to his satisfaction, he never bothered much about any of us. Off to Africa with another crew, with real voyagers perhaps – men! As for Larry, was he even a journalist, I wondered, or a madman and predator masquerading as a scribbler – and God knows there were already plenty of people on Sydney newspapers who fell into that category in those days.

Chapter 2

No picnic at Hanging Rock
(Victoria, Australia)

"**H**OW about doing something spooky? Let's visit Hanging Rock, where those Victorian schoolgirls famously disappeared on Valentine's Day," I said to my travelling companion as we drove out of Melbourne towards the Macedon ranges.

"D'you mean, let's go see how easy it is to disappear up on the Rock?" said Aaron, scornfully, his eyes fixed on the monolithic mound of Hanging Rock that was just visible ahead on the wide bush-covered plain below Mount Macedon.

"Well, yeah. Why not?"

I said it in a jokey way, but I was driven by the desire to do something more adventurous than just tour around the hinterland of Melbourne. However, later on that day, I would feel differently.

I'd been sent by the Sydney newspaper I worked for to interview a well-known Australian actress at a city hotel. Instead of flying back to Sydney on the Friday night, I decided to combine the mission with a weekend break. The decision was easily taken when I discovered the Melbourne photographer assigned for the interview was Aaron, who I'd met a few months previously for another showbiz interview. We got on well over dinner at a Greek restaurant on the evening of the latest interview. Aaron was a handsome guy in that rugged, easy-going manner of Aussie men. He was funny too and a talented snapper, and the friendship had possibilities, despite us living in different cities, more than 400 miles apart.

While we lingered over moussaka and a bottle of Greek wine, an attraction seemed to be developing, but in a casual way, as we'd both recently left long-standing relationships. We were just on the right side of cautious. We planned to meet again the next day and Aaron suggested a trip north-west of Melbourne, where he was keen to take some pictures of the Macedon ranges in the soft early autumn light.

A last-minute photographic assignment had made him late and by the time he collected me in his car, it was mid-afternoon. It wasn't until we were getting close to Hanging Rock, and saw how much it dominated this vast landscape, that the idea of a visit there seemed very appealing. It was a place I'd never had time to investigate before but had read a lot about. I was attracted to the 'fact or fiction?' aspect of the famous disappearance tale.

"Have you ever climbed to the Rock's summit?" I asked him.

"No, and I can't believe I haven't. I've seen the *Picnic At Hanging Rock* film by Peter Weir, of course, but I admit I don't much believe all the stories that've circulated for years about the place, especially all the supernatural stuff. I'd be keen to get some photos though. I've always loved the landscape in this region."

It seemed odd to me that a photographer as talented as I knew Aaron to be had never thought to capture one of the most iconic natural attractions in Victoria. Hanging Rock was the setting for the mysterious disappearance of four schoolgirls and one of their teachers on Valentine's Day 1900, which was the subject of Joan Lindsay's best-selling novel of the same name, published in Australia in 1967, and which the author hinted may have been based on a true story. The Weir film was released in 1975.

As Lindsay's story goes, a group of students and two teachers set off for a picnic from the nearby exclusive boarding school, Appleyard College, named after its owner and headmistress, the prim and controlling Mrs Appleyard. On a perfect sunny day, the group settle in the 'recreation grounds' below the Rock. After a leisurely lunch, some of them fall asleep in the shade of gum trees, guarded by their French teacher, Dianne de Poitiers, but four girls and the maths teacher, Greta McCraw, decide to climb the steeper southern end of the Rock.

Two of the girls in particular, Miranda and Irma, are beautiful, rather ethereal creatures, in their Victorian muslin dresses, and keen for a challenge on a warm soporific day. It is an image that a young well-to-do Englishman, Michael Fitzhubert, and his horse handler will later find hard to forget when the girls trail past, coaxing admiring glances.

A few hours after the group start their climb, one of the girls, Edith, the plainer, frumpier one, returns alone and in a state of hysteria. When asked about the whereabouts of the others, now long overdue to return, Edith can only remember that the last time she saw them they were climbing towards the summit, along with the maths teacher who is (shockingly for 1900), wearing only her underwear.

In the following days, despite a thorough police search of the Rock with dogs and Aboriginal trackers, and an intense investigation, no trace of the three girls and teacher are found, apart from a small strip of dress material spiked on a bush. It's only the further exploration by Michael Fitzhubert, keen to solve the mystery, that one girl, Irma, is miraculously found a week later, unconscious on a ledge near the summit. Although she makes a full recovery, she too remembers nothing of the climb. And so the mystery continues, never to be solved.

The greater mystery surrounding the tale, however, was whether it was vaguely true and based on a little-known historic incident, or just a piece of imaginative fiction. Lindsay, in an author's note in the book, said, rather unhelpfully: "Whether *Picnic At Hanging Rock* is fact or fiction, my readers must decide for themselves." Certainly, there's nothing in the book to help the reader decide, but one event may explain the paucity of real historic detail: the local police station near Hanging Rock reportedly burnt down in a bushfire in 1901 and all files were allegedly destroyed, including the investigation into the mystery disappearance.

The controversy over the truth of the book continues to this day, and the Rock still attracts droves of visitors eager to retrace the steps of the Victorian schoolgirls to the summit, in the hope of solving the conundrum one day. Most swear the place has a creepy ambience. I was attracted by talk of the site having a supernatural feel to it, but apart from that I thought our visit might also be a rather romantic thing to do, with its Valentine's Day association at least, even though we were a month past that date when we visited.

Hanging Rock dominates the surrounding plain and glowers over it, spelling drama from a distance, but in true Australian fashion there's humour to be found in the location as well. A signpost on the approach road had been re-styled by some visiting mischief-maker, or larrikin as the Aussies would express it, who had tied a small rock to a piece of thin rope and hung it from the 'Hanging Rock' pointer. We laughed at the black humour of it and Aaron stopped the car to take a few photos.

However, the Rock itself is no laughing matter. The closer to the base you get, the rough, jagged rock peaks announce something sinister, even on a warm, vibrant day. The peaks are mostly tall and pointed and have been eroded over the centuries to create dark depressions that look like eye sockets and gaping mouths, so that the front of the monolith leers at you like an ancient chorus of ghouls.

"Now *that* looks really creepy," said Aaron as he drove into the car park.

The Rock is 718 metres above sea level but only 105m above the plain. Called a mamelon, the structure is around six million years old, created after an explosion of blistering magma from below spewed out through rock fissures. When it cooled it formed the monumental array of boulders, peaks and rock ledges you see today, leaving also deep bottomless crevices, now surrounded by trees and bushes.

It looks like the younger sister to the more famous Uluru (Ayers Rock) in central Australia, which is 348 metres high, but unlike Hanging Rock was not created from exploding magma. A sandstone monolith, it was fashioned 550 million years ago as softer surrounding rocks began to erode through time, leaving Uluru dominating the surrounding plain. It was sacred to the local

Aborigine tribes who have lived in the region for more than 30,000 years. Since 2019, owing to its status as an Aboriginal heritage site, visitors are no longer allowed to climb it.

We got out of the car and looked up at the Rock, tiny compared to Uluru, which I had climbed years earlier, but the ascent here was no doddle, or so I'd read. And the ghoulish formations would ramp up the effort, I was sure.

"Are you up for a walk to the summit now we're here?" I asked Aaron.

"Sure. And I'm just glad I didn't wear my thongs," he said, using the Aussie word for flip-flops.

"Me too," I scoffed.

He looked at my trainers with a nod of approval but the rest of my outfit made his dark eyes crinkle with amusement.

"I don't know if you're really dressed for climbing, to be honest, but it kind of suits the Hanging Rock theme."

As I hadn't been expecting an afternoon climb, I'd picked a slightly floaty mid-calf skirt, long-sleeved white T-shirt and the wide canvas hat I always wore on hot, sunny days because of my pale Scottish complexion. The outfit was unintentionally reminiscent of a Victorian girls' outing. I was standing by the car with my hands on my hips, frowning.

"Don't worry, we're not climbing Everest. Anyway, I'll get nice photos out of it. You, looking floaty around rocks," he said, with a sardonic smile. I laughed. It was so like a photographer to see everything in life in terms of what looked good in the viewfinder.

He swung his camera bag over his shoulder and we started our ascent, but not the steeper choice of the Victorian school group on the south face. We took a more popular path up a set of rocks that formed a natural staircase, winding up through the gum trees and past thick scrub full of ferns and wildflowers. We passed the signature spot where a massive boulder was wedged mid-way between two soaring rocks, forming a natural low archway and giving the Rock its modern name. However, in the mid-19th century it was also known as Mount Diogenes, after the ancient Greek philosopher, and founder of the school of Cynicism. He believed in stoical self-sufficiency. I wonder what he would have made of this stark, iconic location.

Beyond the archway, the trees and scrub began to thin as we gained height, yet other formidable boulders and soaring rocks loomed over the track, with the signature dark eye sockets and gaping mouths like Edvard Munch's *The Scream*. The place was full of drama and chills and I now understood how anyone could disappear up here, because now and then we passed caves and high pinnacles with deep dark chasms between that seemed bottomless, where a young girl might fall and never be seen again. I shivered. Behind me, Aaron was busy, his shutter clicking endlessly as he took dozens of shots because, like every photographer I'd ever met, a few pictures were never enough.

"I hope you're watching where you put your feet," I shouted. "Have you seen those chasms?"

"Nah, too busy taking pics," he laughed.

"That's not really funny."

"Yeah, you're right, but what's really funny is you in that skirt and hat. You're looking more and more like a missing schoolgirl."

"Don't be cheeky, and don't keep reminding me, or you'll put a hex on us," I laughed grimly.

We climbed further up to the summit, which was not one prominent peak but a plateau populated by more ghoulish rocks and flat rocky areas in between that constituted pathways of a sort. From every vantage point were spectacular views out across the plain and in one direction to Mount Macedon. Most of the pathways led to ledges or low outcrops of rock, with sheer drops towards the plain below.

There wasn't another soul at the top, so Aaron took advantage of our lofty retreat to make me perch in the shade of some of the more disturbing rock formations, as if we were doing a low-budget photo shoot for a fashion magazine, though in reality it probably looked more like an arty spread in Rock Climber's Monthly. It was interesting to see him work, as if we were up here for a serious assignment, him wanting dozens of different angles in different lights, moody or maddening.

I'd always found photographers at work compulsive viewing. I had respect for the way there was usually a strange connection between them and their subjects, like I felt up on the plateau, as if the camera lens is a portal through which someone else has a split-second entrée into your innermost thoughts. Not every photographer seems to have that connection, and not every subject gives up their thoughts too easily. And on the Rock that day I felt unguarded and exposed in a way, and relieved when we'd finished.

We sat for a while in the shade, drinking water from a plastic bottle Aaron kept in his camera bag. It was much hotter on the plateau, even though the afternoon was drawing in. Aaron took off his baseball cap and wiped a handkerchief over his smooth olive skin, which sheened with sweat. I was grateful for my hat at that moment.

"You know, I can't believe I haven't been up here before either. I've had a few assignments in Melbourne over the years, and then there's an unfortunate connection with this place that I didn't mention earlier," I said.

His eyes flickered with interest. "I think you'd better tell me," he said, stretching out on a flat rock with his hands behind his head.

"I interviewed actress Helen Morse not that long ago for a new theatre production she was in. But in Peter Weir's *Picnic At Hanging Rock*, she'd played the French teacher Dianne de Poitiers, remember?"

"I do, and she was lovely, very photogenic."

"I was writing a long profile piece on her and beforehand I was warned by her publicist to absolutely not mention actor Bryan Brown, with whom, you might remember, she was supposed to have had a 'friendship', while they were filming the 1981 mini-series *A Town Like Alice*."

Morse had been a star of theatre and TV from the 1970s, though not as well-known internationally as Brown, who later cracked Hollywood with some decent film roles.

"So, I'd been warned about Brown. Trouble is, telling a journalist not to mention something, just ramps up your curiosity even more. Near the end of the interview, I pushed the envelope and asked her why journos were told not to mention Brown."

"I can imagine what happened then. I've heard she can be prickly in interviews," said Aaron, staring up at the sky.

"I just expected her to say 'no comment' but she went *ballistic*. It was scary. She stopped the interview and raged at me for a while and demanded that someone find her publicist and bring her in to explain. We were in the offices of the Sydney Theatre Company and it just went from bad to worse, with lots of accusations and bad language. It was the most stressful interview I've ever done."

Aaron laughed heartily. "Perhaps she'd suffered, what would you call it, the curse of Hanging Rock while filming up here in the 70s, before she met Brown."

"That's fanciful."

"Well, something was nettling her, that's for sure."

"It's a long time to be nettled and look I'm not sure the Rock ghouls had anything to do with it. More likely it's just the curse of actors getting hung up with other actors," I said, laughing at the memory of that explosive interview, not thinking I'd ever be recounting it at this particular location.

I took off my hat and lay down on an adjacent flat rock, feeling suddenly sleepy with the heat and the chat, and I noticed that Aaron must have felt the same. He shut his eyes and, after a few moments, fell asleep. I gazed up at the cloudless, deep blue sky. From this angle all seemed perfect and serene and in no time I fell into a deep sleep myself, dreaming of Helen Morse having a tantrum amid the chasms.

I was awakened suddenly by a loud scream. A horrible, jarring noise in this creepy setting. I felt panicked and levered myself up onto one elbow and looked around. Nothing. Aaron was still sleeping soundly. I waited a moment and then lay back down again, still unnerved by the noise and the eerie setting. It was only when a flock of garrulous, screamy cockatoos flew overhead, stark white against the indelible blue of the sky, that I sighed with relief.

Apart from the birds, it was quiet on the summit, for an Aussie bush setting, whereas down by the car park I'd heard the insane laughter of a kookaburra, the warbling of magpies, and I'd seen a wallaby scrambling through the undergrowth. Although I say it was quiet up there, there *was* a kind of 'noise' that, subliminally, I'd been aware of most of the way up. Now, reclining quietly on my rock bed, with the cockatoos dispersed, I was able to focus on it properly. It was a strange humming noise, a kind of drone, like thousands of invisible cranky gnats hovering in a cloud.

"Are you awake?" I said softly to Aaron.

"Just," he said, sounding sleepy.

"Do you hear that noise up here?"

He looked over at me, slightly dazed, and shook his head. "What noise?"

I tried to explain what it was.

"You're hearing things. Losing a few kangaroos in your top paddock," he said, tapping the side of his forehead.

I laughed at his Aussie idiom. "Possibly, but listen … don't you hear it?"

He was quiet a moment. "No, I don't," he said with a quizzical lift of an eyebrow.

"Maybe I'm a bit light-headed from the walk in the heat. I should have had more for lunch," I said, thinking of the late, leisurely meal we'd had in a pub in a nearby town, though I'd picked at mine, not hungry then. Now I just felt fuzzy.

"Better get a grip," he said. "We don't want you teetering off the edge of the Rock."

He sat up slowly and rummaged in his camera bag, pulling out a red apple. It looked like it had been bedding down with the lenses and boxed film for quite a while, but I was glad of it anyway.

I talked and ate at the same time, ravenous. "I can see now how you could easily get lost up here, physically or metaphorically. I did read once that like Uluru, this place was sacred to local Aborigines. They are supposed to have used it for a few thousand years, holding initiation ceremonies around the base, and corroborees. But apparently they never came up here, to the summit, because they said it was inhabited by evil spirits," I explained.

"Nah, I don't believe all that stuff. I mean, I've got great respect for the Aborigines and their beliefs, but evil spirits up here? I personally don't go for that. But maybe you've got superior gifts and that noise you're hearing is you tapping into a parallel world. Maybe the schoolgirls are there and they're trying to spook you," he said, laughing impishly, rubbing his hands over sleepy eyes.

"Stop it!" I said, with mock annoyance, pitching the apple core over a rock towards a steep escarpment. It was a spontaneous action and yet the thought of anything falling off the side of the Rock at that moment felt slightly disturbing. I wished I hadn't done it.

We were quiet a moment and then Aaron stood up, ready to continue the walk. "Look, I've heard all the theories as well about the girls disappearing into a time warp, ending up somewhere else, if the Hanging Rock disappearance is true, of course. If it is, I'm just not into all that weird stuff," he said.

"I take your point, Aaron, but this place is definitely spooky in the way old houses are."

"Yeah, well, I'll admit it feels like something not quite right has happened up here, whatever it was," he said.

"I agree and it scares me when *you* say that."

"I'm starting to scare myself," he said, laughing. He looked attractive when he laughed, showing big even teeth and his eyes crinkling at the corners. Not for the first time that day I thought how unfortunate it was we lived so far apart.

We finally set off again, around the plateau. Maybe it was an optical illusion but the profusion of rock formations and clearings paved with flat rocks, and the views out towards the wide plain, gave the summit the appearance of a much bigger, wider space. We wandered around it for another half an hour, with Aaron taking more pictures while I trailed behind, feeling increasingly overawed but unnerved. It was easy enough to forget that time was passing and that we should start our descent before the light began to fade.

Once we'd set our minds on finding the original path we'd come up, however, we couldn't locate it, even though we roughly knew where on the Rock it should be. Every time we moved towards a clearing, or a likely configuration of rocks and trees, we found nothing and ended up walking round and round the same space. We came to a stop in one of the clearings, flanked by a circle of low rocks, like a small bush setting for a theatre.

"Jeez, you know what?" said Aaron, rubbing his chin. "I'm starting to think we could actually be bloody lost ourselves now. How ironic is that? I mean, how hard can it be to find the path we came up on? It's not like we're on something the size of a golf course, is it?"

"I'm thinking that as well," I said, feeling panicky again, as if another screechy flock of cockatoos had just sailed past. "Is this what happened up here, do you think? The girls simply became disorientated and lost and fell down a rock crevice, never to be found?"

"Steady on," he said, slumping down onto a small rounded rock, sipping his water. He took out his mobile, a clunky piece of apparatus, such as we had in the early 1990s. He tried to get a signal. "Nothing, of course," he said, pulling a face. "It's probably jammed by signals coming from deathly portals."

"Maybe it's the gnat clouds," I offered, noticing how the invisible gnats were starting to make a hell of a racket now, not that Aaron noticed.

Then something unaccountable happened. Six other visitors suddenly strolled into the space, like a theatre troupe having heard the right cue. We hadn't heard them approaching, or seen any signs of them previously. For a moment none of us spoke but stared disbelievingly at each other.

There were two young guys dressed in black, like punks, with rows of earrings up their ears, like shower curtain rings. The other four were a family, with two adults overdressed for the heat and two kids aged about 10 and 8. Suddenly, whatever they'd been discussing previously resumed all at once. The punks were arguing about something, and the kids were moaning loudly about wanting to go home, with the mother chiding them. The father came over to us.

"Have you been here long? Are you two lost as well?" he said nervously, looking at us with big watery blue eyes. For a moment it all seemed comical, except there was nothing funny about being stranded on the Rock, and with this strange crew.

"We can't seem to locate the track we walked up. Don't know where the hell it is now," Aaron told the father.

"Same here. We've been wandering about, with these two guys here," said the father, pointing to the punks, who pulled sullen faces, anxious to get back to their even darker normality away from a family of moaners.

The mother was wringing her hands. "I didn't want to come. I told Edgar it was a bad idea, and dragging the kids up here, too."

That was the cue for the kids to lament their distance from home. They droned loudly like a twin-engine plane in a death spiral. The punks were bickering again. I shivered. I felt cold all of a sudden.

"We can't be lost," I said to the father. "I think we're all just fazed by the Hanging Rock story. We've all read the book, seen the film, the whole package, and our minds are playing tricks. Obviously. We all need to calm down."

Aaron gave me a troubled look. He took off his baseball cap and ruffled his thick black hair. Then he got up quickly. "Look, we can't just sit here. I'll go off and search out the path we came up on. It's easier than all of us wandering about. I'm sure I'll recognise the descent track when I see it. You all sit here and wait, right?"

He leaned over and whispered, his lips grazing my ear. "Scream if there's any problem, and mind my camera bag." He nudged it towards my feet.

And off he went before I could stop him from leaving me alone with this group of nutters. In no time at all, the family got properly hysterical once they noticed the orange ball of sun was drifting towards the horizon. Darkness on Hanging Rock. What would that be like? The father was walking round in circles. The kids began to whine loudly, and my gnats were getting screamy too. The punks looked more fed-up and sinister, their earrings glinting orange in the late afternoon light, their short black hair shining like helmets.

The kids started crying, wiping their noses across their long-sleeved tops. I felt sorry for them. I tried to offer soothing words and told them my friend Aaron would find the way down, no worries. But even the punks were getting angsty now as we waited, and waited. It was now about 40 minutes since Aaron had left us. What the hell was he doing?

One of the punks cupped his hands around his mouth, shouting: "Where are you, mate? Bloody hurry up and find the track!" The family started shouting as well. "Where are you Aaron?" and "Don't leave us here alone."(That was the kids.)

It was hard not to think of the Lindsay book again, the mystery over the disappearance, the Weir film, the floaty, sinister quality of the whole thing, ramped up by the Aussie bush which, in the best of circumstances, can seem overwhelming, especially at night, when lizards and snakes might be on the prowl and spiders the size of frisbees quiver in giant nests strung between trees. While there were physical hazards galore up there, I couldn't get the spooky stuff out of my mind, us being pulled into a disastrous portal, into a nebulous time zone when the stars and planets were in some kind of hideous alignment.

It started to make sense to me that the wise Aborigines never came up here. In Lindsay's book, the girls and teacher had simply disappeared off the face of the earth, never to be found. I was sure now that the story was real enough, not hyped-up fiction.

This led me to think of Aaron. What had happened to him now? He must have heard us all shouting. At the start of the afternoon climb, when all seemed well, I decided I'd offer my newspaper a travel piece on the Rock when I got back from Melbourne, using some of Aaron's pictures, but instead I realised I might be writing a piece about his disappearance, if the rest of us survived, and we'd all be part of a sinister movie sequence.

"We can't hang about here any longer," whined the father.

"Yeah, mate, too right," said one of the punks, kicking his black-booted foot against a tree stump.

"I agree," I said, standing up hurriedly, grabbing the camera bag. "Let's at least go and look for Aaron, even though he told us to wait. He might have fallen down one of those horrible crevices." Oh God, this trip had turned out to be such a bad idea. My idea, too.

We started skittering around the plateau, taking rough paths in haste, but the more we took that ended nowhere, or onto dangerous ledges, the more we seemed to be stuck in a giant maze. In the end, one of the punks had a decisive strop.

"This is bloody ridiculous! We can't just wander about like this. Follow us. We'll find the proper way down, okay," he said, his eyes flashing with intent.

"Okay," we said, trooping behind the pair, who didn't appear to know where they were going but they had some swagger about them at least. The family kept up their moaning repartee, the mother dragging the younger boy by the hand, crying buckets again, the father pulling the other one.

"Not that way, this way!" I heard one of the punks shout at his friend several times, with oaths bandied about.

I felt dizzy, like I'd been pushed around a boxing ring for an hour, when finally I heard one of the punks say: "Here it is, must be here."

He turned towards us and jerked a thumb at a wall of rocks and trees. I looked around the backs of the others and there was Aaron, sitting on a flat rock beside a descending pathway. When we reached him he seemed dazed, his camera still slung around his neck.

"Thank God we've found you," I said, bending down, squeezing his shoulder. "I was panicking, thinking you might have fallen somewhere."

I looked around for the others, but they'd gone already, rattling down the path like demented antelopes, kicking up scree.

"Are you okay?" I asked, as I sat on the rock beside him.

"Guess so. I found the path here straight after I left you all. But I feel really spaced-out. Drank all the water," he said, waving his empty bottle.

"But that was 40 minutes ago. Have you sat here all that time?

He gave me a quick, worried look. "Don't know what you mean by 40 minutes ago. I checked my watch when I got here. I'd say it was about five to ten minutes ago, that's why I didn't come for you straight away. I sat here for a breather." He was looking at me oddly.

"Are you sure about that length of time?" I leaned in and checked his watch to see if it had stopped. It hadn't and it read exactly the same as mine.

"Aaron, you didn't leave us about 10 minutes ago. It was definitely more like 40. I know because I kept checking my watch. We were all wondering what had happened to you because you'd taken so long, but we were too scared to set off to find you in case we got into a bigger muddle."

"I did call out for all of you. You must have all been fairly close but I didn't hear anything back. I didn't want to leave the descent path in case I couldn't find it again. But, mate, it wasn't anything like 40 minutes. I mean, that's totally weird. Something's wrong there. Unless I got sucked into one of those creepy portals where you get robbed of time, and then it spits you back out again," he said, with a look of tired confusion.

I laughed to make light of his comment, but there was little humour in any of it. I felt cold and shivery again, despite the fact that the sinking sun looked hot and vibrant on the horizon, like a distant wildfire.

"Come on, let's get down the path. We don't want to be stuck up here after sunset," I said.

He took his camera bag from me and we made good progress down the pathway we'd taken from the car park. Back in the car, we sat quietly for a moment, staring up at the glowering ghouls of the Rock, turning a ghastly indelible orange in the last rays of sun. There were only a couple of cars in the car park, and no sign of the punks or the family. I wasn't surprised.

We didn't talk much as we drove off towards the city. Aaron looked dead beat, like he'd run a marathon. It worried me. Had he tripped and bumped his head, losing track of time, or had he had some other kind of dippy experience amid the myths and mayhem? Whatever had happened, he just didn't want to talk about it.

When he dropped me at the hotel, I persuaded him to come in for a light snack at least and a drink in the bar. He looked like he needed it. We talked about work mostly and avoided Hanging Rock for a bit. I was relieved when I saw he'd started to revive and seemed more like his affable self. After a while we even managed to have a laugh about the excursion. There was nothing else you could do really.

"Typical, isn't it, that the punks, the most confronting of the group, ended up saving us all. Just as well. I think they probably felt like pushing the moaning family literally over the edge at some point, and me as well," I said.

"You know, as I said to you earlier today, I still don't buy into all the other-worldly stuff, but there is something about Hanging Rock, isn't there? I agree it does have an unsettling atmosphere, a presence, you might say, as if the rocks aren't inanimate. I felt like they were watching us the whole time we were up there. Jeez! That makes me sound as crazy as a possum on a pub crawl," he said, laughing tentatively, using one of his colourful Aussie expressions.

At least he still had a sense of humour, but I knew exactly what he meant. I had felt as well that we weren't alone up on the Rock, long before the others sprang onto the scene. And the droning gnats had stopped when we arrived back at the car park. What that was about, I felt I'd never know.

"Maybe the Aborigines were right about not going to the summit, for whatever reason. Maybe those schoolgirls just broke some unwritten law or something, without knowing it," I offered.

We talked a bit longer about other things and while he sounded like his old self there was something in his eyes that was less calm and confident. He went home not long afterwards, saying he needed an early night. He had a big family commitment the next morning.

I felt weary when I got up to my room and had a long soak in the hotel's extravagantly large bath. I raided the mini-bar and sat in bed for a couple of hours watching TV, silly but lively programmes to make me think of something else rather than ghoulish monoliths.

On the plane back to Sydney the next day, I had plenty of time to mull over Hanging Rock, however, and Aaron. So much for me thinking that the outing might progress our friendship a bit towards romance. It was hardly that, but I hadn't known him long enough to be too invested in that notion, and distance was an issue.

As it happened, we were never to meet face to face again. The frisson of attraction I believed we'd had between us disappeared, like the Victorian schoolgirls. I did speak to him briefly on the phone a week later and asked if he could send some of the Rock pictures for my travel piece. I mentioned another interview that might be coming up in Melbourne and expressed the hope we might meet. I was surprised when he told me he was incredibly busy in the coming months and was travelling a bit himself with photographic assignments. The meaning was clear. The idea of us maintaining even the vaguest of friendships was now impossible.

It was curious and inexplicable, given our once-palpable attraction. Perhaps he'd recently met someone else; understandable really. Or perhaps the Rock excursion had affected him in some way that even he didn't understand, and not pleasantly so. Perhaps he blamed me for that, for persuading him to go up there, to "see how easy it might be to disappear", as he'd said jokingly in the car on the way. He had disappeared in his own way. Had we hexed ourselves with our jokey attitude to awesome Hanging Rock? Did everyone who made the trek up to the summit?

I did think a lot about the Rock in the following months and re-read Lindsay's book. In the story, the blonde and ethereal Miranda, the maths teacher and a third girl, Marion, were never found but the Rock's pernicious aura was blamed for other tragedies. One troubled pupil at the Appleyard school, Sara, fell inexplicably to her death from a top-storey window. Later, Mrs Appleyard, riven by guilt perhaps over the Valentine's Day tragedy and the ensuing downturn in the school's fortunes, committed suicide by walking towards the summit of the Rock and jumping over the side, or so it was said.

As for the ones who disappeared, if troublesome spirits had been trawling the summit, perhaps even a scintilla of romance among the peaks jagged at them. The innocent and eye-catching girls in 1900, in their floaty muslin dresses, attempting that climb on Valentine's Day, were surely prime targets for some mayhem. It could also explain why my own bid for romance that day on the Rock slid into the abyss. Was *this* the real curse of Hanging Rock?

A few weeks after the trip, Aaron sent me a few of the photos he'd taken that day, with a short note attached that had an element of finality when he wished me well for the future. They were beautiful pictures, all in black and white, which showed a startling juxtaposition between the grim rocky outcrops and me in the floaty skirt and hat looking happy, without a care in the world. But one of the pictures was unsettling. Aaron had, consciously or not, captured an image of me sitting at the foot of one of the more malevolent-looking ghouls, with its long grey face fashioned from the pits and bumps of weathered rock. It was a horror-show – deep sightless eyes and an open groaning mouth. I pinned it on the wall in front of my work desk to remind me always that even on a glorious day, full of promise, there are dark souls who drift among us, with mischief in mind.

Beside this photo, however, I pinned another one, the comical image of the Hanging Rock signpost that Aaron and I had seen by the road side, with a small rock dangling on a piece of rope. It would remind me of something else, that when life hands you something strange and pernicious, humour puts it all into perspective. Or so I like to think.

Chapter 3
Going troppo in the South Pacific
(The islands of Fiji)

THE tiny island of Qamea seemed to float on the sea, a verdant cluster of palm trees and low hills behind, wreathed in a soft mist. Our motor boat skimmed towards it over clear turquoise water, where the indelible colours of coral were easily visible several feet below. As we drew closer, Qamea seemed uninhabited, the wooden beach huts, or burés, hidden among the trees and an eerie stillness about the place. A lull before the storm, perhaps.

The travel PR taking this group of journalists around some of Fiji's many islands had warned us that a hurricane was heading this way, which was bad news for all the swimming and snorkelling the group planned to do, and trekking to the island's famed waterfalls. On the other hand, there was talk that we might be marooned here for days, a week perhaps, with the incoming hurricane because Qamea was only accessible by boat from the nearby island of Taveuni. No hardship there!

As we neared the dazzling fringe of white sand along the shoreline, the sense of solitude was interrupted by the sight of a welcoming party strolling out from between palm trees onto the beach.

The silence was broken by a loud salutation from the resort's American owner, Dolores, who, according to our travel notes, had marooned herself here about 10 years earlier to fashion her own piece of paradise along this coastline.

Standing on the beach as the bow of the boat bumped onto the sand, Dolores cut a diverting figure, with big blonde hair and a tropical flower behind one ear. She was dressed in the traditional colourful wrap-around sulu and I sensed that at times she injected a lot more levity than was normal into this tropical refuge.

"Welcome, welcome, to our paradise island of Qamea," she drawled, looking like a curvier version of Mitzi Gaynor, who starred in the 1958 Rodgers and Hammerstein film *South Pacific*, the soundtrack of which had been a childhood obsession for a while. I'd played the vinyl record to death for months and knew all the songs. And now, unbidden, the swoony ballad *Bali Ha'i* was playing in my head. Dolores was flanked by two smiley young Fijian women, also in bright sulus, who placed thick flowered garlands around our necks, while *Bali Ha'i* was trilling away, turned up to the max.

"Bali Ha'i may call you
Any night, any day.
In your heart you'll hear it call you,
Come away, come away."

I was close to bursting into song as we were led up the beach to the meeting point at the Qamea Beach Resort, a large wooden structure, *bunckalou,* with a steep thatched roof, like a fringed witch's hat, which had been skilfully hidden in a copse of palm trees and surrounded by flowering bushes.

This was the heart of this small, secluded resort, with its main bar and dining room hung with old-fashioned hurricane lamps, used after dusk. But at that time of day, candles were flickering in the dark corners. The place dripped ambience, less *South Pacific* and more like the location for a moody Pacific tale written by Joseph Conrad. It drew us in immediately.

As we sprawled on the cane sofas, the resort manager, a genial Fijian guy in smart trousers and a bright tropical shirt, brought cocktails in large glasses decorated with flowers. The tropical fruit taste conjured up indolence and mystery as well as a tang of drama to come, and the drinks were strong.

"I suppose you've all heard about the hurricane," Dolores said.

We nodded.

"Don't worry. We're at the tail end of the hurricane season now, so it shouldn't be too bad. But if it is, we can decamp to Naivivi Bay nearby. It's known scientifically as a 'hurricane hole', a kind of natural shelter from hurricanes."

There was a glimmer of fun in her eyes. We all looked at each other, wondering if she was just having a wind-up at our expense. Still, Qamea in a hurricane seemed more compelling by the minute.

The island is just six miles long and about three miles wide and is mountainous in parts. Fiji comprises an archipelago of 330 islands, of which 110 are populated. The two main islands, Viti Levu and Vanua Levu, are home to 87% of the population of almost 850,000 Fijians.

The media group I was travelling with was small: two other female Sydney journalists — Corrine and Cheryl, both reportedly in their late 30s, though I took Corrine to be at least five years older than that — and Joe, 28, a writer from Brisbane, but originally from Cornwall, with a west-country burr that was bound to prove irresistible to the females. Dolores seemed particularly engaged by him and his accent, which she commented on several times. Joe was the youngest in our group, very handsome, with slightly wavy black hair and startling green eyes.

Corrine was the more garrulous of the team, tall and poised, with long auburn hair and a throaty laugh. She was a newspaper travel editor, who had spent more of her life on airplanes, or drinking daiquiris beside infinity pools, than she had at her computer terminal back in Sydney. Everything she wore looked to have a high-class label, and if not always the real thing, her clothes and handbags were perfect clones, the kind of items you could easily pick up in South-East Asian cities in the early 1990s – one of the perks of regular travel. She had a swag of good stories that I expected would keep us well entertained when the hurricane rattled in.

Cheryl was a feature writer on a women's magazine, but with the intention of becoming a full-time travel scribe, her plans for which I'd been privy to at length on the flight from Sydney. She had messy, mousy-coloured hair and there was a faraway look in her big grey eyes, as if dreaming of the next destination, and it had taken her no time at all in our earlier visits to the larger Fijian islands to pick Corrine's brains about travel gigs.

Noah, the airline travel PR, was a pleasant, almost shy man in his early 40s, who wore striped shirts and well-pressed chinos and shorts that gave him a no-nonsense air, which was appealing after my experience with previous travel PRs, such as Jason in Kenya, a man I would not want to share a hurricane with, especially if there were wild animals stirred into the mix.

After cocktails and a light lunch, we had the afternoon to ourselves, with the evening meet-up in the main building set for 7pm. We were each given a self-contained, thatched buré facing the sea. Noah's buré was closest to the main building, the women's in a row, and then Joe's slightly further up the beach. Perhaps Dolores had sensed sexual frisson in the air after one look at Joe, and put him further away from the rest of us, for his own sake perhaps. She seemed to have the instincts of an elephant sensing an imminent tsunami – or in this case a wave of tropical infatuations.

The palm trees were set at regular intervals in front of the burés, very tall, very commanding, their thick fronds giving the appearance of wild, sticky-out hair. A long sentinel of these trees also leaned right over the beach, as if guarding the compound. On the walk to my buré I noted the hand-painted signs attached to every half a dozen trees: "Beware of falling nuts." At first I laughed, but when I tried to visualise the outcome of a coconut escaping from a high cluster and landing on your head, I was less amused. For the most part, like someone obsessively avoiding the cracks in pavements, I avoided walking under the trees.

The burés ramped up the sense of being marooned in paradise, with their high thatched roofs, wooden canopy beds, shutters, rattan ceiling fans and no telephones or TVs. Perfect. A siesta in this tropical cocoon would have been remarkable after the day's journey, but I had a mind to swim before the storm blew in. I changed into my costume and slipped into the warmest, bluest, gem-like waters I'd ever seen, outside of the Greek islands.

I swam up the beach and found Corrine dog-paddling about elegantly in a designer one-piece, her hair piled on top of her head and fastened with a huge tortoiseshell clip. She was wearing bright pink sunglasses, clearly not dressed for anything athletic. In a costume she seemed chunkier, big-boned, and busty with it. It was curious to find her lapping around the sea opposite Joe's buré – or perhaps not. His buré was quiet and shuttered, and I imagined he was fast asleep.

We made small talk as we paddled about and I mentioned Joe in passing, naughtily prying to see if perhaps a holiday fling might be brewing in tandem with a hurricane in this exotic location. On the trip so far I'd seen them chatting together, but I hadn't seen romance blossoming yet, possibly because, as with most media trips, the first few days were packed with scheduled visits (on the bigger islands) and schmoozing with hotel PRs. Qamea was supposed to be a chance to really unwind in Fijian fashion.

As for Joe, Corrine seemed surprisingly firm. "Oh, good God, he's too young for me! And I'm in the midst of a messy relationship with a married doctor. I don't think I can deal with coitus among the coconuts right now."

I laughed. It was the kind of dippy thing she sometimes said.

"What about you? He's not too young for you I think," she said, narrowing her eyes at me. I don't know what she based that on because I was no younger than the other women, but I let it go for fear we'd talk on and on about poor Joe, as if we were haggling over mangos in a rural market and whether they were ripe enough to eat.

"Nah! I'm not tempted by media-tour romances. They seem a bit naff to me," I said rather piously, but with good reason. I cringed when I thought of the vile creature who'd cottoned on to the women on an African media trip I'd taken just months earlier, who would likely have bedded anything as long as it had a blood count.

Corinne raised a questioning eyebrow at me, as if she didn't believe for a moment that I didn't indulge in up-and-away affairs. Australian media trips, for the most part, had always had the reputation of being a hot-bed of sex among the scribes, like sailors let loose in foreign ports, who might think their deeds won't catch up with them. Mostly they don't, but Sydney was a small place then in most respects and sexual exploits among journalists made for lurid late-night stories in the city pubs that serviced the newspaper industry.

I'd never met Corrine before, though I'd read her travel features. But now I could sense that despite her current reservations, there was an aura about her of foreign trysting, of a superior nature, of course. Or perhaps it was my imagination ramped up by the tropics.

In the early evening, our group gathered in the bar for pre-dinner cocktails and then moved to a round wooden table, lit with candles, for dinner at 8pm.

We were suitably dressed for the occasion in smart summer casuals. Only Corrine had made an extra effort in a vibrant fifties-style dress with a generous reveal of cleavage. Noah was smart and corporate. Joe was handsome in a crisp white shirt and casual trousers. Cheryl was missing.

"Where's Cheryl?" asked Noah, wrinkling his brow and looking around the table, as if he'd only just noticed she was an hour late.

"No idea," said Corinne, looking at her watch. "She did say she was going to have a nice long nap. But, honestly, this is bad-mannered, isn't it?"

Dolores smiled indulgently. "She's on Qamea time, hon. That's what happens to you here. I used to be like that too before I had a resort to run."

She called the Fijian manager over and asked him to knock on Cheryl's door, as there were no phones in the rooms. We ordered dinner, as we were all starving. As soon as the entrees arrived – spicy pieces of fish with mango, wrapped in some kind of tropical leaves – Cheryl turned up in a flurry of apologies. She'd overslept and had left her alarm clock at home. But we weren't listening to her excuses, we were side-tracked by her outfit. She was wearing the colourful sulu, with its vibrant tropical prints, that we'd all been given as a resort gift, to be used, we imagined, as a beach wrap. Hers was tightly wrapped around her slim hips, like an ancient Egyptian winding sheet. The outfit was completed with a crisp white T-shirt, a flower behind one ear and jangle of tribal beads around her neck.

"You look, em, very Fijian," said Corinne, giving her a strange and amused look.

"Well, silly me," said Cheryl, taking a large gulp of wine. "I packed in a bit of a hurry and forgot to put enough smart clothes in my suitcase. I'll have to improvise." It was clear that Cheryl was charmingly scatter-brained and I wondered what improvisation might mean to her. Dolores was thinking along those lines as well.

"Don't worry, hon, I think you'd even look sensational in the Fijian grass skirt that we wear at *mekes*, the song and dance ceremonies. I've got a few spare here, if you'd like one," she said, with a sardonic twitch of an eyebrow towards the rest of the group.

Corrine laughed lightly into her entrée. Noah sipped some wine and stared at the hurricane lamps lit around the periphery of the room.

Cheryl wasn't bothered. She seemed to have fairly thick skin. "Grass skirts, eh? Don't temp me now, Dolores! I've been known to wear some outlandish outfits in my time." I didn't doubt it.

Joe, who had been rather quiet up to now, suddenly broke cover, remarking with a boyish gleam in his green eyes: "Well now. Grass skirts usually don't come with a top, so you could fashion yourself a coconut-cup bra to go with the outfit, like you see in old movies."

"South Pacific," I offered.

"Exactly," Joe said, waving his fork at me.

Everyone turned to Joe in surprise because he was never one for idle nonsense or the sly salacious comment. He was a country boy, brought up on a sheep farm near Bodmin in Cornwall before emigration to Australia called and the lure of journalism. Everyone laughed over the coconut bra, except for Cheryl. She was staring with intent into the middle distance, as if mentally constructing just such a bra for her next dinner occasion. I wouldn't have put it past her.

Noah seemed unfazed by our sometimes cheeky girlie banter, but whenever he was, he would look away and affect a sudden and comical interest in the room's exotic décor. New to the job as a travel PR, he seemed to be still learning the ropes and was happy to let everyone indulge their own fantasies, while making sure we stuck to most of the rules.

Conversation was light during the rest of dinner, with its offerings of Fijian specialties based around fish and seafood, but also a chicken dish in a creamy curry sauce. We soon began to feel the effects of a long day and a few too many glasses of wine. Dolores filled in every lull in the conversation with colourful anecdotes about her life and why she'd first come here on holiday.

"Well, it started with a romance with a cool guy from San Francisco, who I was crazy about. I thought he was going to pop the question. But then he broke off the relationship for someone else, just like that!" she said, snapping her fingers.

"So you brought your broken heart to a paradise island," offered Joe.

"Yes, honey, I guess I did." Dolores gave him a look as sweet as a pineapple cocktail.

Bali Ha'i was momentarily abandoned. I started to hear the first bars of *I'm Going to Wash That Man Right Out Of My Hair,* sung by Mitzi Gaynor after a romantic kerfuffle.

"I ended up here and just fell in love with the place," Dolores explained. "There were a few small settlements on the island 10 years ago, but nothing on this stretch of coast, apart from a couple of abandoned shacks and the remains of the temple building that became the dining room we're sitting in. I told the tour operator I was coming back as soon as I could sort out my finances and that I was seriously going to build a small resort here and stay forever. For a gal on her own, it was a big undertaking. Crazy, I guess!"

I was sure everyone agreed with her last comment and were probably also wondering, as I was, how she had financed this foreign fantasy. No-one prodded for information. It seemed immaterial.

"I so wanted this place to be palm trees with a view. I wanted visitors to walk lightly on this piece of paradise. No big development, no speed boats, no razzmatazz."

"Not Florida then," Joe piped up with a smile.

"Oh, hell no, honey!" said Dolores, with a hearty laugh that pinballed around the wooden rafters.

One thing was sure during dinner: Joe was proving to be a slow burner and showing a bit of cheek in his charming Cornish way. Or was he just coming over all Qamea? I could see that Corrine had similar thoughts, and she gave him an admiring glance or two. Not so young for her now, perhaps.

Before we set off for our burés that night we could feel the first push of the hurricane. Rain started to patter down and the wind was rippling the palm trees.

As we walked along the narrow path back to our rooms, I thought of those falling coconuts. If they had a mind for dropping, tonight was the night, and there would be plenty of coconuts for Cheryl's bra construction!

I lay awake in bed a while, listening to the rising wind and rain and feeling nevertheless rather excited by the prospect of spending more than the planned next two days here.

In the morning, the storm was more intense, the waves were rolling in with white tops and the palm fronds en route to the dining room were having a lively strop. I hugged the path close to the line of burés.

We stayed in the main building after breakfast and read newspapers a few days old and chatted, while the hurricane gathered more power. Dolores had the radio on and we listened to regular weather updates. There was no TV reception here apparently.

Noah knew we were all hoping to squeeze out an extra day or two here. "Guys, be careful what you wish for. A hurricane on these islands could cause huge devastation. We don't want that, do we?"

Dolores didn't seem fazed at all. I guessed that once you've hitched yourself to a tropical island for life, you're well prepared for anything.

"Don't worry, y'all. According to weather reports, we're still on the edge of the hurricane, not in the eye of it, so it will blow through soon enough," she said, soothingly.

We stayed for lunch and gathered again round the radio. It was quite dark, so Dolores lit the old-fashioned hurricane lamps. It was cosy as we spread out on the cane sofas, drinking coffee and eating local pastries that were a speciality of Dolores's chef, originally from Suva, Fiji's capital. We told travel tales and laughed over some of the strange and ridiculous things that happen to journos on media trips.

Sometimes just being a journalist in certain locations is enough to spice up your whole trip. I remembered again my previous trip to Africa with Jason, when he was petulant and irascible at having only women in his group. After Kenya, we had four days in Zimbabwe. Jason had warned us that on the arrival forms for immigration we were absolutely not to put down that we were journalists, and to say we were a group of friends travelling around Africa.

"Be creative, say what you like, but if you put journalist, you'll be whisked off for questioning, and I don't have time to stay behind and sort it out. I've got an itinerary. Zimbabwe is averse to any media scrutiny at present. And whatever you put, you'll only be given about a week's stay anyway, which is fine. And for God's sake put something down you know about," Jason had moaned. "You'll be asked questions. I mean if you put ballet dancer, make sure you can really do a pirouette. The guy checking your details will probably ask you to perform one. Trust me."

It had all seemed a bit of a joke as we sat on the plane filling out the forms, racking our brains for plausible professions. One of the group settled for psychotherapist, another for ornithologist. Jason was getting angsty and told us it would probably end in disaster.

I decided to put 'artist' on my arrival form. My mother was an amateur painter and I'd watched her often enough.

How hard could it be? I thought. The irascible Jason had scoffed at my choice. "I just hope you've got an easel with you, dear," he said, with a curl of his lip.

When we got to passport control, our forms were taken and we were all lightly quizzed about who we were. Jason had squirmed the most but ended up putting down the obvious – travel specialist. I was quizzed about what I was painting. Lions, elephants, natives, I babbled. It sounded weak to me but the immigration officer was unaccountably pleased that I might show his country in an optimistic light and stamped my passport with great relish. While everyone else got their measly week's stay, I had been given six months in Zimbabwe, which amused me, and I waved my passport stamp under Jason's nose, feeling enormously smug.

"I hope passport control asks to see some of your African masterpieces on the way out," he quipped sarcastically.

While we waited for the hurricane in Fiji, everyone had a story to tell, whether it was having to eat strange and disgusting food in exotic locations, or being ill at the wrong time, or making a fool of themselves in different cultural situations. No-one had much to say on the latter category, but that was yet to come on this Fijian trip.

During the night we felt the full force of the edge of the hurricane, with the crazy lashing of palm fronds and the wind beating at the witches' hats of the burés. Would they withstand it, I wondered, as I cowered in my bed, glad this was only hurricane-lite. What would a real one be like?

The next morning the rain and wind continued but it had less bite than the previous day. The paths were littered with palm fronds and the odd coconut, one smashed to pieces, oozing its juice and a mush of bright, fragrant pulp.

Better on the path than on someone's head, I thought. The sea was churned to a milky green without its turquoise lustre.

Noah announced that we would be able to leave the island the following morning and I felt disappointed at not having another opportunity to swim here, around the vibrant coral outcrops.

I was sorry to leave, as a few more days would have been perfect. I doubted I'd ever visit a place so lush and remote, cut off from the mad frenetic world beyond it, and that was even in the days when our lives weren't as proscribed and dumbed-down by the internet and social media. What would Qamea seem like today? Like a refuge on another planet?

On the morning we left, it was sunny and steamy warm. As I walked down the front steps of my buré, ready to take the short narrow path through the palm trees to where a small boat was ready to pick us up again, I felt revived and relaxed.

I stopped for a moment to get my camera out of my bag. And at that very moment, a giant coconut released itself from its vertiginous cluster and fell with a sickening thud onto the section of path I was about to take. I stared in panicky disbelief. It's not how I would have wanted to bow out of the island, or life for that matter. So paradise had a dark side after all. The errant coconut was still intact. I picked it up and carried it down to the beach, where the media group had gathered. Dolores was hugging everyone goodbye. I gave her the coconut and explained my close call.

"Oh, hon, but you were damned lucky. So, I'll keep your coconut to remind all my visitors to take the signs seriously about the falling nuts," she said, hugging it to her chest, which gave me a thought.

"Actually, Dolores, I think you might want to take Joe's advice and fashion a coconut-cup bra for some future fashion initiative," I offered.

"Good thinking," she said, with a minxy smile, looking towards where Joe was standing, flanked by Corrine and Cheryl.

As we waved goodbye from the boat, the island became a shimmering, floaty mass again, the palm trees along the shore swaying lightly in the breeze, as if waving farewell. It was a cue for Bali Ha'i to start up again. The earworm had taken root:

"Try, you will find me,
where the sky meets the sea.
Here am I, your special island, come to me, come to me."

I'd found my own special South Pacific island, and from here it was back to a different kind of Fijian reality, which was no hardship at all, of course. The other smaller islands in the remote north of Fiji also had an allure of their own, such as nearby Taveuni, where our boat took us back to. This is called the 'garden island', with a rainforest and an extinct volcano that still feels very off-grid. The main islands, Viti Levu and Vanua Levu, have a different vibe and a mix of cultures, particularly along the coastal areas, from Fiji's commercial past and the descendants of European plantation owners. In the Fijian capital, Suva, on Viti Levu, there are streets sporting grand colonial architecture and Victorian-style parks built for the great planter families, and a mix of cuisine, religion and culture.

Fiji was first populated around 3,500 years ago by tribes from Indonesia and the Philippines. Throughout its history it has had a tight band of communities with a strict hierarchical and patriarchal structure, relying on the cultivation of indigenous fruit and vegetables, such as cassava, copra, sweet potatoes, papaya and pineapple. In earlier centuries cannibalism was widespread, though it was finally stamped out by the 1830s due to the arrival of Christian missionary groups.

When Europeans began exploring the Pacific, the Dutch first sighted some of Fiji's islands in 1643 and then William Bligh, commander of HMS Bounty, sailed through the islands in a long boat after the infamous mutiny on the Bounty in 1789.

By 1860 the islands were attracting European settlers keen to establish lucrative cotton plantations, for which they brought in thousands of Indian workers, who later remained in the country, along with other Indian migrants, which created long-running ethnic tensions in later centuries. Fiji became a British crown colony in 1874 and while economic development burgeoned, the country was wracked by periods of political power-play between the various groups. A push for independence started in the 1960s and Fiji finally gained independence in 1970, after 96 years of British colonial rule. Parliamentary elections were finally held in 2014.

From the island of Vanua Levu, we flew back to the Viti Levu, staying in a resort south of Suva, the purpose of which was a visit the next morning to a traditional working village on the banks of the Navua river. It was marketed as a unique village experience. It was certainly unique — but mostly for the wrong reasons.

At a pier on the banks of the Navua river, we were met by a young Fijian guide tasked with taking us upriver in a longboat, with an outboard motor at the back, just big enough to accommodate the five of us. We'd been advised to dress in smart but sensible summer outfits. However, Cheryl as usual chose to heed her inner fashion minx by opting for wide-legged cotton trousers with a Polynesian vibe, a long top and fashionable straw hat. Corrine wanted to be seated in the bow, and Cheryl squeezed in beside her.

Noah sat behind them and Joe and I were asked to sit together behind him to balance the boat. Balance the boat? What? Would this be a light kind of white-water rafting experience, I wondered. I had tried this once in Queensland, and it was a terrifying judder and shriek over jagged rocks in a fast-flowing river, like being trapped endlessly in the rinse cycle of a washing machine.

As we cruised up the river, gently to start with, it was all rather pleasant, the steep-sided hills slipping past us, covered with thick jungle vegetation. But as the boat picked up speed, it created a steady spray over the prow from the muddy dark river. I understood then why we'd been told to also bring light, preferably waterproof jackets, which none of us had, except for Noah. I'd expected rain on the hills perhaps, but not this.

Within 10 minutes we all felt the spray but the two girls up front were struggling to keep dry and Cheryl's hat had flown off her head, funnelled away on a firm breeze with no hope of recovery. Joe and I smirked at each other, feeling rather pleased we'd been asked to sit behind the others. Noah, always the gentleman, offered the two girls in front his rainproof jacket to cower under.

An hour upriver and further inland, the expedition started to seem rather gruelling; it was now hot and steamy on the water and muddier the further we went, though a slower pace at least had lessened the spray. With another half-hour to go, my mind wandered. I was momentarily over my *South Pacific* obsession. I'd gone past musicals and was on to books set in tropical hell holes. *Heart of Darkness* came to mind and Marlowe's trip to the Congo in search of the feral Kurtz. And Evelyn Waugh's satirical classic *A Handful Of Dust* wasn't far behind, the tale of a British aristocrat who goes missing on an expedition to the Amazon rainforest and becomes victim to the schemes of a crazed foreigner with a book fetish.

Namuamua village, when we finally arrived, seemed a quiet settlement of simple wooden buildings on a narrow plateau beside the river. Most of the village was skilfully hidden amid the trees, despite having a few hundred inhabitants.

A modest contingent of villagers met us at the wooden pier: the chief, some of the elders, and a few young men and women, who we were told would join in the *meke*, a Fijian song and dance performance, after lunch in the communal hall.

Before we could proceed to the heart of the village, the chief insisted on sorting us into the requisite hierarchy: men first, women trailing behind as befitted the male-dominated society here, although it was done with certain levity and much giggling from the village children, who'd tagged themselves onto the procession.

After a light lunch of fish, salad and tropical fruit, we were taken to the community hall, a modest building with a pitched ceiling and small windows to keep out the sun. For the *meke*, the women were dressed in their colourful sulus, the young men in the grass skirts Dolores had referred to. They were bare-chested with ornamental garlands around their necks. The chief wore the grass skirt but with a patterned shirt and small headdress and sat at the front of the proceedings, the men and women on either side of him, sitting on the floor.

We sat in one long row in front of them, further down the hall, to give them performance space. Having seen a few *mekes* on our tours so far, we expected it would start slowly and end perhaps in a mad conga line, as it had on one occasion, though I doubted a conga line struck the right chord in this isolated spot. Before the *meke* started, the chief gave a short welcome speech in a loud, deep voice as two young women appeared from a side door carrying a large wooden bowl and several smaller ones the size of cups.

We were to be offered a bowl of kava as part of the chief's welcome. I heard Corrine sigh beside me. I gave her a quizzical look. She leaned in and whispered in my ear: "I tried kava once. Don't drink too much, okay."

We hadn't imbibed it on the tour so far but I'd read about in some of the promotional material we'd been given. It's a drink known locally as *yanggona*, made from the roots of a South Pacific plant and drunk widely in the region. Though not alcoholic, it's said to have sedative, euphoric and even anaesthetic effects, which struck me as a dubious asset, but potent, at any rate.

The kava was distributed by the women and, apart from us, only the chief and elders were handed kava as well. As the chief wound up his welcome speech, I was handed my bowl. I looked down and saw liquid the colour of the Navua river. Not as appealing as one of Dolores's mai tai cocktails. As the chief quaffed his, we sipped. It tasted like mud, earthy, thick. I thought I was going to gag and struggled with the reflex by resorting to a few verses of *Bali Ha'i*, my go-to stress-buster.

"Come, my friends, drink up!" the chief boomed. "It is our gift of friendship to bless this occasion."

Corrine nudged me and stage-whispered: "Just keep sipping. Don't gulp it."

"As if!"

Noah, in the middle of the row, gave us a silencing look, which was not his usual style, and said as quietly as he could: "The kava's fine and, by the way, you do have to drink most of it, if you can." No pressure then!

It's one of the unwritten laws of any media trip that you have to try everything, whether you want to or not. Food (witchetty grubs, barbecued crocodile); daredevil sports pursuits; stroking snakes in tropical zoos, drinking kava.

I sipped a bit more, not with great relish, but mercifully the more you drank, the less you seemed to taste it. And there was a reason for that because while we watched the vigorous *meke* — the women singing sweetly and tapping sticks on small wooden drums, the men doing some kind of warrior dance that shook the floorboards — our mouths started to go dry and numb. The anaesthetic effect kicking in? We all remarked over it and were beginning to feel slightly numb all over and sleepy from the crowded, stuffy hall.

Corrine, however, seemingly forgetting her earlier reservations, finished off her bowl of kava and was curiously into the dancing and singing, jiggling her shoulders, flapping her hands to the ceremonial beat. Too numbed perhaps for clapping. It was all very curious, and when my kava was finished — leaving a slick of mud at the bottom of the bowl — and the *meke* was ending, I thought, *Okay, no harm done.* But the entertainment hadn't finished.

"Now something more to your taste perhaps," the chief said, with a deep chesty guffaw. I was sure he was referring to his drinks menu. A whisky and soda perhaps, or a G&T, if that might even go with kava. But no, he had something else in mind. Worse! Much worse! He wanted to see a 'happy disco' with western-style dancing. Tropical hell!

"Everybody to get up now and dance," he commanded, summoning the young Fijian locals and warriors onto the dance floor. Corrine was less enthusiastic now, as if dancing while seated was preferable. But Cheryl suddenly leapt up, ready for some fun. What a dark horse. Where did she get her stamina?

Two young men fetched guitars and strummed tunes that seemed to be Fijian mixed with early western pop classics, which was strange and oddly unnerving. We were embarrassed at first, so the chief got up and elbowed some of the young men and women to partner us on the dance floor, which they did timidly, like teenagers at a school dance.

It was hot and airless in the hall and the kava had really kicked in now in weird ways. We started dancing around, improvising, while the locals did a peculiar version of sixties' dance moves: the pony, the jerk, their grass skirts flailing, their chests sweating. My partner was young and eager and the frantic swish of his grass skirt at least provided something of a cooling breeze. But in no other way was this enjoyable.

Other villagers, at loose ends, piled into the back of the hall to watch and I realised finally that this crazy performance in a sleepy village, upriver, so far from the modern delights of Fijian towns, was probably fashioned for *their* entertainment entirely, rather than ours, but in a benign way, surely, not an Evelyn Waugh, hell-in-the jungle kind of way.

All the same, we were dying on the dance floor, apart from Cheryl, whose arms were flailing everywhere but whose legs, in her droopy wide trousers, were moving heavily, like a weightlifter's. It was bizarre. And we all looked the same, dancing with arms possessed, but dragging our feet.

It was as if kava made you 'drunk' from the legs up, and your head would likely be the last thing to shut down, unless you got lucky and just fell on the floor catatonic, and didn't have to dance any more — or live, more likely.

I'd never seen anything quite like it — and I don't want to, ever again.

After some 15 minutes of this, while Cheryl's arms were still jittering and angsty, Corinne, whose partner had finally taken refuge with a few other warriors at the back of the hall, was now beginning to buckle.

"I've seen tipsy goannas look saner than we do," she groaned as she treacle-walked past me. Noah, I noticed now, was dancing like a man on puppet strings, opposite an attractive local woman, who was trying to match his erratic movements with her own, and failing. She finally gave in to an eruption of giggles, which set me off as well, as much as you can giggle when your throat's numb.

With her partner gone, Corrine staggered over to Joe as the music strummed on and the heat increased. Through the madness I could see the chief was still smiling, totally oblivious to the state we were in. *When will this dance torture end?* I thought. But I kept going, coaxing my legs about the room, dripping flop sweat, and feeling queasy in the stomach. Corrine and Joe began to slow dance, which in this frenetic set-up seemed radical.

Corrine was wrapped tightly around him, her head on his shoulder, looking swoony. So, love in the time of kava was my dizzy thought as I felt the blood drain abruptly from my head and I collapsed onto the dance floor in a sorry heap and had to be helped outside by Noah.

On the front porch, I staggered away from him. "Gotta go," I slurred over my shoulder as I moved to the side of the hall out of sight and threw up lunch and kava into a bush. After a few breathless moments, I felt like a new woman, like ancient Aphrodite born out of the antediluvian mud.

Noah appeared, looking panicked, and fanned me with a travel brochure.

"Are you okay?"

"Yes, don't worry. Much better now. Kava. Horrible stuff. Never again."

He sighed and fanned me a bit more.

"I agree. Didn't quite know it would be that potent. First time for me too. Sorry… But I'm sure the kava wears off quicker than you imagine."

For someone new to the travel game I wondered at his confidence in these things. No matter. I had at least expurgated the fiendish brew.

"Will you be okay here? I'm going back into the hall to try to round up the others. By my calculations we should be leaving soon," he said.

I leaned against the side of the hall, listening to the indescribable musical melange going on and on. That's when I thought again about *A Handful of Dust* and how Tony Last had been kept prisoner in a remote jungle village by Mr Todd, a crazed Brazilian/British expat, who forced Last to read aloud every book in his voluminous Dickens collection. The prisoner was drugged each time an escape opportunity arose. It had to have been kava, I was sure of that now.

I hoped Noah had told the hotel where we were going for the day. My mind started to blaze with daft paranoias, when abruptly the music stopped and our media group came wobbling outside. The chief and elders were none the worse for the entertainment, and mercifully didn't seem to notice that we were looking green and delicate. However, the chief ordered someone to bring us cooling slices of fruit on a big platter and glasses of water before our return journey.

Now whenever I think of Namuamua, I'm convinced there ought to be police fines for drink-jiving on tropical shores.

The boat trip back to the hotel was a sleepy blur and the seating had changed this time, with Corrine and Joe at the front, Cheryl behind and Noah and me in the back row to balance the boat. No-one complained about the spray from the bow this time or how long the journey was taking. We were heading in the right direction, that's all we knew.

Back at the hotel, Noah told us that as the next day was our last in Fiji, we were free to do whatever we wanted. Only Cheryl and I opted for the pool and I had no idea what the others were doing, which was all for the better.

When I went down to the restaurant the next day for breakfast, I found Joe sitting on his own at our group table, drinking coffee. He looked a bit weary, hair ruffled, eyes red-tinged. I asked how he'd slept.

He sighed. "I fell into a deep sleep but I woke up feeling tired, just like I did the day before. Must have been some residual effect of the kava. God, what fiendish stuff that was!" he said, with a comical grin before slugging some coffee. Ah, bless him, I thought, and it was a good try, playing the ingenue so sweetly.

"The others are late," I said. "It's typical of Cheryl, but not Corrine, is it? She's usually the first down." The Namuamua slow dance had been the precursor for a passionate night or two, I imagined. Who could really blame Corrine?

I gave him a probing, minxy look. He didn't take the bait, though his lips daintily puckered. His version of 'no comment', perhaps. Then he quickly changed the subject.

"Any idea where your next travel trip will be?" he asked.

"Not a media trip. Not for a while, but I'm keen on a holiday back in Scotland."

"Ah, that'll be a change of pace then?"

"Yes, it will. Apart from the kava incident, this has been a fabulous trip. But strangely, I'm feeling rather nostalgic for my homeland, for cold lonely glens and baldy mountains. I'm even craving a few wailing bagpipes."

"Yeah?" He looked briefly amused.

"What about you? Back to Cornwall sometime? I hear it's rather lovely."

"It is lovely, but I'm not quite done with tropical adventures yet, if I get another media trip that is. Though today I do feel a bit travelled-out."

"Hm, I can *well* imagine," I said, playfully sarcastic. He gave me a shrewd look and sighed, almost painfully. Seems I'd overplayed the Corrine hand.

"Have you had breakfast already?" I asked him, feeling suddenly quite hungry.

He shook his head.

"No point in waiting for the others," I said, getting up and heading for the buffet. I heard him trudging along behind me. While I poured myself an orange juice I watched him scoop tropical fruits into his bowl and a large dob of yoghurt, then he sprinkled nuts on top, seeds, dried fruits in small squares, shreds of coconut. It seemed to go on forever. A tower of goodness.

"Healthy breakfast," I commented, and then I walked to the other end of the buffet table for some fresh bread, cheese and cold cuts. When we got back to the table, he sat for a moment contemplating his bowl, as if his appetite had momentarily flagged.

He leaned towards me slightly and said in a soft voice: "Can I just say something to you?"

I stopped chewing and nodded, intrigued at this hint of intimacy.

"I know what you're thinking, and the others probably, that Corrine and I have a thing going on now, a kind of troppo kava slip-up. Yes?" he asked, in a tired kind of voice.

I gulped down a mouthful of cheese. "Em, well, I don't think ...."

He cut me off. "I assure you we're NOT," he said, with emphasis, spoon in hand now, toying with his fruit and nut tower.

"That's okay, you don't have to explain."

I was surprised at his confession but not heavily invested in the end about what they might or might not have got up to.

He continued: "But the thing is, if I can quote a wise scribe, 'I'm not tempted by media-tour romances. They seem a bit naff to me'." He winked. "And I don't do coitus amongst the coconuts either – not yet anyway." He guffawed, looking more lively all at once and taking a few mouthfuls of his breakfast.

He'd just quoted the comment I'd made to Corrine while we swam outside his buré on our first day on Qamea island, as well as Corrine's coconut quip.

"You cheeky monkey!" I said, my face flushing with embarrassment. "You weren't in your buré that afternoon. You were sloping about behind the palm trees and bushes, eavesdropping. Or maybe you'd set up a palm-cam somewhere nearby?"

"Oh, that's a good one. Never thought of that," he said, his eyes sparkling with mirth.

I gave him a long searching look. Joe was amazing really. Behind the boyish charm he was actually a lot smarter and shrewder than anyone guessed. I imagined him in Qamea that day strolling out of sight near the beach, having a good laugh at two media women talking absolute tripe, with him taking notes, photographs too perhaps. Would it all end up in a story one day?

I didn't speak for a while, quietly finishing my breakfast.

"Sorry. I didn't mean to offend," he said, his head tipping sideways in a gesture of mild repentance, though I wasn't sure if the gesture was a mocking one or not. I chose to think it wasn't.

I shook my head. "Joe, I'm not offended. I know you're a decent, sensitive kind of guy, and everyone on the trip likes you, but with reference to my comment: you see, people go daft on media junkets and do things that are totally out of character. And shag a lot, I might add. Happens all the time. But good for you for being the smart one," I said, smiling. My face was still burning with shame, but I was impressed he'd been classy enough not to become a media junket cliché. He didn't need to. I was sure of that.

"I was just taking your advice after all." He patted me lightly on the shoulder and then dug his way through his bowl of goodness.

When Corrine finally strolled into the dining room it became clear the reason for the sleep-in was quite different from what I'd imagined, and that a drinking session in the bar the night before with Cheryl had gone on a lot longer than expected. I could see it perfectly in my mind: the cocktails flowing, Cheryl plundering contacts and career opportunities from Corrine's long back-catalogue in travel. No matter. I had never been on an Aussie travel junket yet that was ever just about travel. In the frenetic and sometimes glamorous world of modern journalism, how could it be?

I laughed heartily. Joe shot me a rather fetching and knowing look.

* * * * *

Fiji had been a revelation: a tropical smoothie of calmness, chaos, and coitus interrupted. I took three things back with me: 1. The earworm of *Bali Ha'i,* which continued at intervals like a South Pacific fever and then disappeared completely one day, never to return. 2. A growing admiration for cute and forthright Cornish men. A trip to Cornwall was definitely on the cards one day. 3. The realisation that even in paradise you could possibly die slowly on a dance floor from the feet up; or suddenly, under the palms with a ripe coconut landing on your head, ending your tropical bletherings for ever. There are no shades of grey in paradise.

Chapter 4

Hysterics in the heather
(The Hebrides and Highlands, Scotland)

THE road to Ullapool spooled out under a leaden
sky, threatening rain. Celtic rock music boomed
from the hire car's sound system, a mix of ramped-
up reels, moody ballads and, occasionally, blaring electric
bagpipes. It matched the scenery perfectly.

I'd bought the cassette tape that morning from a
roadside tourist shop. It was atop a pile of others on the
counter, along with the shortbread and fudge, and the
ubiquitous small woollen sheep with stick legs that pass for
a highland souvenir. I'd never heard of the band, Wolfstone, or Celtic rock music, or the fact it was one of the
hottest bands in Scotland at the time. None of this, however,
was the least bit appealing to my passenger, my mother
Mary, who was with me on this sentimental journey back
to Scotland, from our current home in Australia.

I turned up one of the tracks as we were about to crest
a hill. The bagpipes swirled around the car like a

demented battle cry. Mary gave me a cartoonish look of fright.

"What's that awfie noise?"

"Electrified bagpipes, Celtic rock. It's a cool thing now in Scotland," I replied.

She shook her head. "Och, away with you! That's just daft bagpipes, surely. Anyway, I never thought you liked any bagpipes."

"In a small burst, not the long bagpipe assaults we used to have every New Year in Australia." I smiled to myself, thinking about the annual Hogmanay parties my parents put on in our backyard, which neighbours couldn't have liked very much, but no-one had the nerve to complain about. Not that it was all bagpipes. There were the old classic numbers from groups like the Alexander Brothers, with twee lyrics like *"I'm Sandy. I'm Andy. Two highland lads are we!"* which my cousins and I mercilessly took the piss out of.

As the car reached the top of the hill, something unimaginable happened: the music seemed to roll out across the scene ahead of us like a film soundtrack, so that you couldn't imagine one without the other. We were heading into a wide glen with a river to the left and vacant, brooding hills rippling off to the horizon, with long-passed stories patched into them of everything the Scots have ever loved and lost. Here it all was – and the music.

The next track, however, was a ballad, and that too seemed perfectly stage-managed and hit its stride with a mournful guitar riff, as heavy clouds began to drift over the hills, where here and there I noted the skeletal remains of once-grand fortified towers and castles.

Mary was quiet, her eyes gleaming at the view. Nostalgic silence. One of the things Scotland gives you, in muckle big buckets, is nostalgia. It's stitched into the scenery wherever you go. Unavoidable.

"This is gorgeous, isn't it?" I waved a hand at the landscape as we started our descent.

"Aye, it is. I'll give you that."

"Worth coming for?"

She nodded.

"And there's more like this where we're going. And a few surprises."

"What surprises?" she asked, her eyes flickering towards me.

"You'll see."

Returning to Scotland for a holiday with my mother had been my idea. Although we'd been back separately since my father died years earlier, we'd never come back together. She'd turned 70 and while in reasonable health and young looking for her age, I wondered how many more times she'd be able to take the long flight from Sydney to Scotland, the homeland she'd never lost her affection for, despite decades living in Australia. This was one journey we wanted to make together while we could still manage it, and it promised to be more adventurous than my mother's usual trek back to the familiarity of Perthshire, where we'd both been born and where she still had some distant relatives and friends.

"Let's see more of the Highlands, the west coast, the far north. The scenery will be spectacular," I'd told her when I first suggested the trip.

I thought she'd relish the chance to have a guided tour, as it were, to far-flung Scotland, but she wasn't keen.

"I've seen the Highlands," she'd sniffed.

But I knew she hadn't been further north than Inverness, and never to the far north.

The Highlands would be rain-soaked and dreich, she moaned, as is often the case in Scotland, even in late spring/summer. But in the end she agreed. Two weeks or so, driving north from Glasgow and stopping where we fancied. In those days, in the mid-1990s, internet booking of hotel rooms or B&Bs was unheard of, so you couldn't plan ahead without a faff. In any case, I don't much like plans. I like to be a freer spirit.

Mary was also an easy-going soul generally and we got on well, with a bond forged mostly after my father died suddenly of a heart attack in his fifties, a tragedy that would weigh on her happiness for the rest of her life. But how the pair of us would get on, up in remote corners of Scotland 24/7, I couldn't be sure. We'd never had such a long holiday together in recent years. It would be a trip to remember, one way or another.

I had loosely decided on taking in the west coast through Ross and Cromarty and then Sutherland, that wild and remote north-western corner of Scotland, and then east to John O'Groats and down to Inverness. That was as far as my plans went, though I had a few other options mulling about in my head.

In Ullapool, I booked a twin room in an old pub near the waterside. The village sits on the northern side of Loch Broom in a spectacular, remote setting surrounded by mountains. The village was established in 1788 as a fishing port, mostly herring, and it's still the main industry in this part of the north-west Highlands. However, the area also attracts a healthy number of tourists keen to tackle the stunning mountain trails and particularly the munros (a mountain over 3,000ft) on the Fannich and Beinn Dearg ranges to the south.

We had a pub meal downstairs after we arrived and the place was packed for a weekday evening. The village is famed as a centre of arts and music, with a strong leaning towards Gaelic culture. A group of local musicians had gathered in the centre of the main bar, which I was told they did every week. There was a fiddler, flautist and singer, and we passed a few hours after dinner enjoying the entertainment.

"No electric bagpipes here, you'll be pleased to know," I told Mary, who was sipping at her malt whisky on ice.

"Praise the Lord for that then!" she said, with a mocking smile.

It turned out to be a great night and I got blethering with a few locals, who were keen to know about our touring plans. I told them, as far as they *were* plans. One young lad suggested we should detour before heading north and go to the Outer Hebrides, catching one of the regular ferry services across the Minch, the sea channel, to Harris and Lewis.

"It's another world over there," he said. "You have to go."

I glanced at Mary to see if she'd heard our conversation but she was talking to one of the singers taking a refreshment break. I had toyed with that exact idea of the Hebrides before we left Glasgow and it was one of the wee surprises I'd mentioned, even though I'd swithered over it a lot in the previous days. I thought it might prove too much for my mother, who didn't like sea crossings much. But just hearing the words "it's another world" and I was smitten with the idea again, or else I'd had too many whiskies.

When I woke up in the morning, I made up my mind to organise a crossing to Harris and Lewis. I left Mary in the room after breakfast, while she was packing, and nipped out to book ferry tickets on the Caledonian MacBrayne service for the afternoon. I was confident she'd enjoy it in the end.

"So where are we heading today?" she asked, as I loaded our suitcases in the car boot.

"Now, don't be alarmed, but I've decided we should have a few days on the Outer Hebrides," I said firmly, as if it were beyond discussion.

"What? You mean Harris and Lewis over the Minch?" she said, as if I had suggested rowing out to St Kilda, the deserted island even further into the Atlantic.

"Yeah, what do you think? We'll never get the chance to do this again."

"Well, that may be true, but I don't much like sea voyages, you know that," she said, her lips puckering with displeasure.

"It's only a three-hour journey." I pulled the tickets out of my bag and showed her.

"So it's too late to say no, isn't it?"

It was a gamble buying the tickets first and my heart sank at the possibility she might refuse to go. To be honest, Mary, for most of her life, had never been one to shirk adventures. In looks and outlook she always seemed a good 10 years younger than she was. As a child I was told she'd been quite a tearaway, up for any prank. Yet here was a dalliance too far perhaps.

"I've heard about the Minch, how it gets right choppy out there in the middle."

"Not always, and anyway the weather's fine today," I said, soothingly. That's always a delusion in Scotland, of course, because the weather can turn on a sixpence. The cliché of 'four seasons in one day' is absolutely right.

She fiddled nervously with the poppers on her padded jacket as she stared out over Loch Broom towards the open sea. I was spiked with guilt.

"What do you think then? Are you up for it?

"Och, why not," she said finally. "I might never come back to Scotland, who knows, eh? We came for some adventure and we've had the scary mountain roads, the doolally bagpipes, now a sea voyage to the edge of the known world. Why not?" There was light sarcasm in her response and a hint of feigned amusement in her hazel eyes.

The only thing to be sorted before we shipped out later that afternoon on the car ferry was to book a few rooms for the three-day trip, one in Stornoway and then further afield. In those days there was scant tourist accommodation on the Outer Hebrides and I was warned at the CalMac ticket office to book rooms ahead at the tourist information office in Ullapool – or we'd be sleeping every night in the car!

The crossing started off under a blue sky with scudding clouds. We stood on the deck a while because beyond the mouth of the loch the view expanded behind us towards the mountain ranges and the peaks we would pass later on our way north, including soaring Suilven, with its distinctive rounded peak. Later, in the ship's lounge, we felt the calm water of the Minch begin to transform about half way across and become choppy. At its roughest, the water seemed to broil, the waves pitching in different directions at once, and the ferry began to roll a bit.

The Minch, between the Outer Hebrides and the north-west coast of Scotland, is said to be one of the most dangerous bodies of water around Scotland. Around 12,000ft deep and subject to strong currents, it can at times become extremely rough, though I hoped not on this trip. As with the west coast of Ireland, the Minch has spawned legends of mythic Celtic sea creatures, most with a comic edge. In this case, the creatures were the Blue Men of the Minch, or Storm Kelpies, resembling mermen with long tails. The blue men have been embroiled for centuries in fanciful stories of dastardly attempts to sink passing ships.

I was glad we'd only had a light lunch before leaving Ullapool because I saw a few greenish-looking faces on passengers after they'd indulged in a heavy late lunch on the rolling ferry. It was early evening when we reached Stornoway harbour, with the welcoming sight of neat white houses around the port and the spire of a nearby church.

Stornoway, the capital of Harris and Lewis, is a small town, established in the 18th century as a fishing port. Gaelic is still largely spoken there as the first language. It was a rather reserved, quiet place back in the 1990s and we were reminded by the landlady at the pub where we stopped for dinner that it was as well we wouldn't be there on a Sunday, or anywhere in the Outer Hebrides, because as a place that has always had strong religious observances, shops and pubs would be closed.

We had a good meal, however, and a glass of wine to toast our adventure before setting off to look for the B&B. The pub landlady gave me instructions on how to get to the simply-named Eilean House (Island House), on the edge of the town. Stornoway isn't a big place, but even with the tourist office map, after driving around for a while, I was no closer to finding Island House. The streets were dark and deserted, apart from one old guy ambling up a long road, leaning forward as if into a strong Atlantic wind, which was probably the default position here.

I stopped the car and leaned over to the passenger side window to get his attention. He gabbled at me a while and I realised he was speaking Gaelic, with words that sounded soft and musical. But I had to cut him short and asked him again where we could find our guest house.

"Aye, I know the Eilean," he replied in English, with a similarly soft and appealing lilt to it, as I was to hear in most of the Hebrideans we met. "Now, I live not far from it but, you see, it's an awkward place to find. Best thing is, you give me a lift up to it and I can walk home from there."

He climbed into the back seat and it became evident he had a few drinks under his belt. It was a shrewd way to get a lift home, but I'd have been stuck without him.

When we pulled up at the Eilean, a net curtain twitched and the front door opened soon after. I'm not a great lover of the British guest house, or B&B to be more exact. Over the years, I've had innumerable uncomfortable lodgings with poor rooms, terrible food and scant service of any kind. Even when everything was passable there was always an eccentricity about the owners that seemed to go with the turf: talking too much because, in essence, guests are a captive audience. Stuck at breakfast trekking your way through mounds of low-density lipids in the cooked breakfast, there's nowhere to run and hide, and that's usually when the blethering starts up in earnest.

Then there are the pernickety owners who are efficient but give you the sense that you're there purely to inconvenience them, make them cook for you, take up half their house, make a mess, and then leave. You can never forget in a B&B that you have invaded someone else's home.

The Eilean in Stornoway was curiously different. And so was the owner, Mrs MacKinnon. She was standing at the front door as we approached, with an affable smile, dressed in a Fair Isle cardigan of earthy colours, with small pearl earrings twinkling at her pink lobes, and tightly curled hair.

"I see you've already met my neighbour Mungo," she laughed. "He's right good at finding a lift home after a night at the pub."

She ushered us in and led the way to our room so we could put our bags down before we saw the rest of the house. We could easily have just gone straight to bed, as the trip on the Minch had wearied us. I'd booked one double room, which was all I could get at the last minute, and when the door swung open we were suddenly wide awake. We were expecting the usual dreary chintzy décor, not this!

Mrs MacKinnon noted our surprise. "The bridal suite, I call it, dears, but it was all I had left, and the tourist office was adamant you'd have to have it, because there was nothing else. So here we are," she said, sweetly apologetic.

The room was a shiny white lace and satin space, like a luxury padded cell, with everything co-ordinated: bed cover, cushion, curtains. The walls were decorated with prints of sunsets and seascapes. Even young newlyweds might have felt their breath catching in here, like being engulfed in a hillock of lavender bags, with the resulting affliction of shy coitus, or something worse.

Mary stood for a moment at the door, staring at the décor, while Mrs MacKinnon explained the rules, hours, where the toilet, kettle, fire door was. I glanced at Mary and she had a look I knew very well, a bottled-up, puffy expression, the precursor to a fit of giggles.

I once suffered this quirk of hers, memorably, in a Tai Chi class a few months after my father died. Neither of us had done Tai Chi before but it was my idea to go along, too, for moral support, hoping that the exercise class would get her doing new things with new friends. The routines were very precise and so slow there was no chance of breaking a sweat. Ten minutes in, and after severe wobbles and arms and legs in a mess, Mary burst into a fit of giggles.

My mother was a veteran giggler, who never failed to set me off as well in those typical situations where giggling is out of the question, like at the opera or in church. I could remember many events since childhood that had brought us dark looks from other participants, but with the Tai Chi, sadly, we were thrown out of the class for ruining the serene ambience. "You no laugh in Tai Chi.

No good!" shrieked the Chinese instructor, as she frog-marched us out of the community hall.

But the giggle reflex passed when Mrs MacKinnon offered us tea and shortbread in the lounge, a homely room that was more the usual guest house style. Later, lying in our double bed, having piled all the satin cushions onto a chair, we had a laugh about everything.

"Jings, this a wee bit over the top, isn't it? I didn't imagine there'd be a big demand for honeymoons in Lewis," said Mary.

"Me neither," I replied, little realising that this would be the first of many strange abodes on this Scottish sabbatical. We slept soundly until a gentle tap on the door next morning reminded us that our big Scottish fry-up was ready, and to be fair it didn't disappoint.

Lewis and Harris, while they sound like two islands, are actually joined and together are 60 miles long and about 20 miles wide. Lewis, to the north and the larger of the two, is mostly a wild, treeless and dramatic expanse, comprised of peat moorland and the rich machair grasslands and dunes of the west coast. Around the island there are more than 1,000 freshwater lochs and, in the centre, craggy peaks. There is little arable land on the islands, with most land used by crofters for growing oats, barley, turnips and for grazing sheep and cattle. While fishing on the west coast and around Stornoway had offered an alternative industry on the islands, over the decades it has declined and tourism is now the island's main concern. Harris has some of the world's best white-sand beaches, surprisingly, such as Luskentyre and Seilebost, tucked away on the south-west coast, which are often compared to Caribbean or South Pacific beaches.

We motored around Lewis for most of that first day, using the map given to me by the tourist office in Ullapool, with places circled that I was told not to miss. But everywhere there were distractions to check out and hinder us, though not unpleasantly so, like flocks of sheep on the narrower roads. In a pub, where we stopped for refreshments, we were entranced by hearing a group of older men talking in Gaelic and a younger man singing in Gaelic, in a sweet voice as pure as crystal, a heart-breaking ballad, I imagined, of lost love or emigration.

Finally we reached the much-lauded standing stones of Callanish, or Calanais, situated near the sea in south Lewis, overlooking Loch Roag and small Bernera island beyond. The stones, like great jagged teeth, are set in a loose circle around a huge centre stone, at the foot of which is a chambered burial cairn. The stones are often described as a smaller version of Stonehenge but these have a different vibe altogether, set on wind-swept moorland, drawing you into past narratives of the folk who lived here in antiquity.

Made of ancient Gneiss stone, some 3,000 million years old, Callanish is said to date from the late Neolithic era (Stone Age) and had been used for some ritualistic purpose in the Bronze Age. The site is on a swathe of land on the west coast of the island that offers a wealth of ancient monuments, including stone brochs (small towers), and there is evidence here of many ancient settlements. The Callanish stones were excavated in 1856 from under five feet of peat.

While we strolled about them we saw a visitor walking with more purpose, a clunky-looking mobile phone (as they were in those days) in his hand, holding it up to the sky and muttering in an American accent. He told us with some exasperation he couldn't get a signal for his phone inside the circle.

"Goddam, but the circle seems to be jamming the reception!"

Mary furrowed her brow. "Why not step outside the circle then?"

He laughed. "That would seem logical, Ma'am, but, I'll be damned, I just want to know why it won't work in the circle."

"The stones have mystical cred," I offered.

Mary decided to give him a gentle reprimand. "Does it matter if the phone doesn't work, unless you're about to have a heart attack and need to call an ambulance?"

"Curiosity, that's all," he said, almost apologetically, as he marched away, still aiming his mobile at the sky, oblivious perhaps to the beauty around him.

Before we left I gazed around the site and wondered at its treeless aspect, like much of Lewis. Apparently, the Vikings were said to have cut down or burned forests of birch, rowan and pine some 1,000 years ago, for reasons we can't be sure of. While the Hebrides, with its remote windswept vibe, doesn't seem like the kind of place to be overtaken by waves of invaders, throughout history it has. The Druids and early Christian missionaries came to do religious battle, as well as stricter Calvinists, with the formation of the Free Church.

Bruce Sandison, in his book on the Outer Hebrides, *The Heather Isles,* says: "Throughout history, there has always seemed to be someone, self-righteous or otherwise, willing, ready and anxious to tell the people of the Hebrides how they should lead their lives." From Norway, Inverness, Edinburgh, London, or more recently Brussels, Sandison says that despite the efforts of these do-gooders and conquerors, "the fact the islanders have managed to retain their identity, sanity and pride speaks volumes for the Hebridean character; welcoming but cautious".

On the way back to the north of the island, we stopped to look at another of Lewis's curious tourist attractions, ringed off vibrantly on the Tourist Board map. The traditional croft houses at Arnol, on a ridge not far from the sea, offered a rather unique and sometimes troubling conduit to the past. Called blackhouses, they had been part of an ancient settlement some 2,000 years old, though the current stone houses date from the 1800s. While many lie in ruins now, walls with views only, No 42 has become the Blackhouse Museum and is kept in much the same style as it was when the last owners left in 1966. Though the place had been refreshed several times since by its then owners, Historic Scotland, it left nothing in doubt about the fortitude of island Scots.

The museum house was a traditional stone structure, very low-slung, with double thickness walls and only one small window at one end. The roof was thatched and weighted down with stones hanging from ropes, which I imagined was to stop everything lifting off in a fierce Atlantic storm. In shape and function, the blackhouses of Scotland are said to resemble the dwellings of Orkney's Neolithic settlement at Skara Brae.

Built in 1875, the last family to live at No 42 was a large one, a few generations together and Gaelic speakers. The house was safe and warm against the storms and bitterly cold winters, but function rather than comfort seemed to be the prevailing theme. Inside, it was divided into living quarters at one end and the animal byre at the other.

The living area had a 'sleeping room' and 'fire room', with heavy furniture, and in the middle of the room was a 'kitchen', a simple peat fire on the flagged floor, with a blackened pot for cooking hanging from a chain above. In the sleeping area were box beds, deep shelf constructions built into the wall, which to the modern mind seem claustrophobic.

When we arrived at the house, we were met by the museum guide, a cheery woman dressed in the spirit of

19th century Lewis in a long, plain crofter's dress and woollen shawl. We stood by the fire, which was lit, while she gave us a feel for what life would have been like for its residents. But within minutes we got the point exactly when clouds of acrid, peaty smoke enveloped us, burning our eyes and throats. As there was no real chimney in these dwellings to draw up the smoke, it oozed upwards and disappeared slowly through the thatched roof, creating black soot around the interior, which accounts for the traditional name.

"This area around the fire would have been the centre of life here. Family and friends would gather here each evening and talk, or perhaps sing," said the guide.

"How did families manage in the heart of winter, cooped up for hours around the fire, with all the smoke and no windows?" I croaked, flapping the peat smoke from my face.

"I know how you feel. The peat smoke affects everyone the same. I'm used to it, and the families would have been used to it, believe me. In years gone by, there was really only peat for fuel, unless you were lucky enough to be able to buy some coal from visiting ships. Everyone cut peat from their land, and people still do hereabouts," she said in her soft island accent, hugging her shawl tightly around her chest. "But in harsh island winters this place would feel safe and cosy. That was the main thing."

Mary rolled her bloodshot eyes at me. I got what the guide was saying, that the house would be safe, warm, with a good bit of craic going about, as the Hebridean people are considered affable, social people. But cosy? After a day in the fields, especially in winter, returning to one of these houses, crammed in with the whole family until morning, especially when it was blowing a hooley outside, with only one tiny window to view the world, cows shuffling at the other end of the house, and the stink of animal manure, wasn't cosy. It made the Flintstones from Bedrock, in their people-caves, seem positively privileged. But this way of life could have been no worse than living in a Glasgow tenement, in poverty, as my father did as a child, with a long stint in the RAF Regiment in the Second World War as his 'great escape', though plenty of poor Lewis men had been lured into the same 'escape' too.

As I thought about the museum experience, however, I realised that keeping the peat fire going for visitors was a brilliant move. Without it, and the unbearable smoke, it was just a nostalgic, forgettable space, like many a worker's rural cottage in 19th century Britain. The peat smoke was a trigger, it elevated the visit to another level, and in the end you felt nothing but admiration for your fellow rural Scots of past centuries and their tough life. You felt their pain, and understood why so many of them chose to emigrate from the late 18th century – if they weren't run off their land first during the infamous Highland Clearances.

Some 10 minutes in and we were both coughing like crazy, with tears rolling down our faces. Mary legged it out of the tiny front door. I swiftly followed and found her leaning against the outside wall, rubbing her chest.

"I think the house needs some of those oxygen masks that fall down from the ceiling in airplane emergencies," she said, with a mischievous red glint in her eyes.

As we walked around the rest of the settlement, looking at ruined houses, you felt that location really was every-thing here: the green moorland rolling down to the sea, a loch sparkling in the distance, and the sense of the natural beauty and fierce independence these proud islanders had, at least some of the time.

We left the blackhouses and drove to the spectacular setting of the Butt of Lewis, at the northern-most tip, with its 19th century brick lighthouse facing the wild expanse of the Atlantic. It ramped up the sensation of being at the edge of the known world, with high cliffs and screaming sea birds. While we were there, the weather started to change, with a smirring rain, typical of Scotland, a gossamer soft rain but cold and soaky all the same.

The tourist office in Ullapool had booked us into a guest house for two nights, a stone farmhouse several centuries old in a spectacularly remote location, a short drive south of the Butt of Lewis, on the coast with moorland behind it. The property had been renovated tastefully, with only four guest rooms, though most of them had sea views, and it was close enough to hear the waves pounding the shore all night.

By the time we checked in and had a quick shower, we found that dinner was already in progress, rather earlier than we'd expected. The dining room had a cracking sea view, and was set up with one long communal table where all meals were eaten. The couple who ran the place, Ted and Shirley, were originally from the north of England. The husband served meals, the wife was something of an amateur chef, and both were quite punctilious with it.

The regime each evening was a gourmet, five-course meal, which I knew we couldn't manage. Even three courses would have been a stretch, so a cut-down menu was negotiated for the two of us before we went into the dining room. I feared a night of possible food torment. But the torment, as it turned out, was to come from a different quarter.

We were hungry enough, however, after a full day of touring. We had changed into smart casual outfits, but with a nod to the salubrious menu, Mary insisted on wearing a set of pearls with her fuchsia-coloured jumper. There had been no time for hair washing and I feared we probably still had the reek of a peat fire on us, and certainly our eyes had stayed a shade of pink, all of which was unfortunate.

When we sloped into the dining room we found a very well-dressed older couple seated at one end of the table, tucking into their first course of lobster. Mary raised a quizzical eyebrow in my direction because she wasn't one for fussy social gatherings, let alone rich food. The couple sounded posh and well-connected, the man in a crisp white shirt and tie, the woman in a silk blouse and tartan skirt, a nod to the host nation, no doubt. I almost felt sorry for them. They probably imagined they'd be having the dining experience all to themselves when we hadn't turned up on time. It was clear from their mutual frowns they weren't overjoyed to share the table with strangers.

I felt weary after a long day of driving and didn't relish conversation with strangers either but realised it was impossible for us all to go through the meal and not communicate. We exchanged pleasantries and brief details. The man was a retired businessman, the wife a doyenne of vague charitable exploits. The pair flinched when I said I was a journalist, but that wasn't uncommon, in my experience, often in those with something to hide. Or otherwise from a dogged misapprehension that all journalists, even on the best publications, are on the criminal spectrum.

Mary and I quickly learned over dinner that the couple, from south of the border, were on some kind of high-brow tour of the Highlands and islands, and probably one of them had a gnarled Scottish root or two to motivate them. I let my mother chatter on about our trip so far, which I found interesting. She had her own take on everything, particularly her description of the bridal suite in Stornoway, which was amusing. The couple smiled indulgently but I was sure it wasn't the kind of Scottish commentary they were seeking.

After our bowls of vegetable broth, our main course of Scottish lamb, was delicious, with a steamed pudding for dessert, all washed down with a few glasses of Italian wine. Near the end of the meal, the couple fell into companionable chit-chat between themselves, until Mary started up about touring mishaps and mentioned the blackhouse visit and our peat fire torment. I expected that if they hadn't already visited the house they'd give it a big body swerve now.

Mary had always been an affable person and chatty, as I well remembered from my early years growing up in Australia. There was a naturalness about her and she had an eagerness to talk to anyone, whether they were fish-wives or flashy aristocrats, chatting in shops or buses. She frequently came home with amazing life stories she'd gleaned, which always made me think that if life had dealt her a different hand she would have made an excellent journalist. On this occasion, the wine had also made her inclined to chat, but I didn't expect the way the conversation would go.

"Of course, I didn't really want to come to the Hebrides at all but my daughter jumped it on me in Ullapool." That was another of her endearing quirks, a tendency to say exactly what she thought, often for devilment.

"Indeed," said, the woman, putting down her pudding spoon and looking at me over the top of her gold-rimmed glasses, somewhat disapprovingly.

"No, I didn't want to come," Mary repeated. "The Minch, I'd heard about it. Don't like boats terribly much. We emigrated to Australia in the sixties, six weeks on a ship, like a holiday camp in some ways. Food was terrible. We all had to sleep on deck, crossing the Equator. It was steaming hot. That was enough for me."

The man cleared his throat and I tapped Mary's foot with the tip of my own under the table, sure that the couple were not the least bit interested in '10 pound Poms' as we were called in those days, the British migrants lured to Australia for a paltry sum. At least they weren't forcibly exiled, like so many Scottish islanders in the past. Mary pulled her foot back and gave me a dark look.

Where was all this all going, I wondered? Even Ted, who was replenishing the wine, lingered a moment, bottle in hand, ears cocked.

"No, I didn't want to come at all! ..." Dramatic pause here. The male diner sighed. The woman fiddled with her gold locket, "... but, you know what, it's been so interesting. Different. Another world, as they say. I never would've come here if I hadn't been press-ganged into it." Mother winked at me across the table, and then laughed merrily.

"Shame about the doolally bagpipe music though. That's a *sair fecht*," she said, firmly.

"A struggle," I said, translating the last part for the couple.

Somewhere nearby I heard Ted laugh softly.

"Bagpipes?" asked the man.

"Ah. My touring soundtrack," I offered. "Wolfstone, Celtic rock. Are you acquainted with that kind of Scottish music?" Cheeky of me to ask because I knew they absolutely wouldn't be. To their credit they looked interested, briefly, and then they managed to shut down the conversation quickly, for fear of where it might lead, by remarking on the variety of Scottish cheeses on the platter that Ted had just brought them. Not long after our desserts, we retired to our room.

We lay in our twin beds a while, our stomachs full, listening to the wind that was up a notch now and raking through the machair, the waves wrecking themselves on the shore line. We talked about the evening and the couple.

"Proper pan loafy," said Mary, making me laugh. The expression means posh in Scots dialect.

"You're right but I felt sorry for them really, being lumbered with us. We wouldn't be their usual dinner guests and there they were, probably thinking they'd have a quiet dinner to themselves, and then we breezed in, all smoky and red-eyed."

"Well, they're not our usual dinner mates either," she sniffed.

"I don't know why you had to say what you said ... about me press-ganging you into coming here! I didn't really," I said sullenly, thinking how to other folk it might sound like elder abuse.

"Just having a laugh," she said.

"But it sounded like you're still not sure about this leg of the trip, even though when we're out and about you seem to be enjoying it."

"I *am* enjoying it," she said, with emphasis, turning towards me, her eyes glassy with slight indignation in the dim light. "Didn't I say it was an interesting place. It is, and full of new wee experiences."

After a heartbeat of silence, she added: "My eyes are still nippy. The guide at that blackhouse could do with handing out gas masks."

I had a daft picture in my mind then of folk standing round the fire in masks, staring into peaty flames and trying to thrash out the notion of 'cosy'. I smiled to myself, but underneath Mary's comical quip, the fact she seemed to appreciate our adventures was welcome – or was she just being a stoical Scot?

Sometimes you can know someone your whole life, and love them absolutely, but it doesn't mean you can get the full measure of them. As affable as my mother was, there were layers to her that I knew I'd never be able to peel back, as there are with all of us. She'd had a hard life, living as a young woman through World War Two, losing her father at 14 and then the hardships of the post-war era in Perth, as her widowed mother struggled to support four children.

Australia had been my mother's bid for a better life, but not before the early years of homesickness, and crying at the dinner table, often comically so, over the poor standard of 'British' food in Australia. She would girn over the lack of a good Scottish sausage or bacon on a bap. Yet we also regularly ate piles of delicious seafood and tropical fruits we never knew existed before we arrived there.

How well I still remembered it. Despite that, I had no idea how she really felt about Scotland itself now, even on her holidays back to Perth, mostly. I felt the trips salved something in her soul and yet she was always glad to be back in Australia, the land she had grown to love, notwith-standing the poor-quality sausages.

"You forget how good it is to have the sun on your bones," she'd always say the minute she landed at Sydney Airport.

Lying in bed, I said: "As for Harris and Lewis, we've only got one full day left anyway, so let's enjoy it."

"Aye, don't worry, I will," she said before falling into a deep sleep.

I lay awake a moment, thinking of the mainland and the trip we planned to take up through rugged Sutherland to Durness, on the far north coast, a swathe of highland Scotland I'd never seen and knew would be on the wild, remote side. Would it have been better to cut that short and take her back to Perth earlier, to spend more time with friends and family (albeit slightly distant)? But then I rejected that idea. No, this is what we set out to do, have a proper Scottish highland adventure. Mary would never get the chance again, I was sure. And that proved to be the case.

Mercifully, we had the breakfast table to ourselves because the other couple had got up early, taken their meal long before us and left. We had a leisurely breakfast while I planned what we were doing that day. The wind of last night had died down considerably and Ted told us it would be sunny by lunchtime. That's Scotland. The weather's a bit like the people, tempestuous or dour for a while and then it's all change.

"There was quite a swell last night. I could hear the beach getting a right pounding," Ted said as he placed a steaming bowl of porridge in front of my mother.

"That'll stick your ribs together," he told her, with a wink in my direction.

She liked porridge the traditional way: thick, and with salt. It reminded me of stories I'd heard about years gone by in Scotland, particularly among crofters, where porridge was poured into a drawer to set and then later cut into squares, like a kind of Caledonian fast food. The thought of it made me feel sick.

Ted hovered round the table. "So, what are your plans today?"

I told him we were driving to Harris to see its famous beaches.

"If you have time this morning, do walk down to the beach here, in front of the guest house. There were big waves in the night and you might find that some ancient bones have been exposed."

Mary's eyes flicked up from the porridge bowl. "Exposed from where?"

"This whole coastline here was once an Iron Age settlement with forts and brochs, which were big dry-stone structures. And burial sites, of course. People were buried in cists made of stone slabs. The shoreline here's been worn away over the centuries and the graves were once much further back, but now with coastal erosion, after rough seas the cists become exposed in the bank at the back of the beach. We found the contents of a cist about a year ago and had to call the police out, as you do when human skeletons are discovered, even if you think they're ancient."

Mary rolled her eyes at me and licked the last smear of porridge off her spoon.

"Do you think we might want to do that then, look for skeletons?" she asked me, with a frown.

"Och, it's not grisly," said Ted "They're old bones. When the archaeologists finally arrived here after our call-out, they also found some artefacts and Iron Age jewellery with the bones, and the whole lot was taken away for examination."

"That's exciting, but do you seriously think we'll find another exposed cist?" I asked, becoming interested. The idea of Iron Age valuables sparkling amid the sand was appealing. It would make for good copy for later, either for my own paper, or for a freelance travel piece.

"Maybe, but even if you don't, the beach is grand and you will enjoy the view right out to the Atlantic."

After Ted went back to the kitchen to fetch our cooked breakfast, I asked Mary if she was up for a nice beach walk.

"Well, I can just sit in the lounge and read a magazine, I'm not bothered. But I'll come down if you want."

"Good, let's go down then."

We wrapped up in warm coats and hats, as the wind was calmer but a bit cool. The path to the beach was easy and the long stretch of white sand was deserted and pristine, except for a thin line of seaweed washed up overnight. All along the hinterland of the beach the wind toyed with the machair, the wild grass that is prevalent in western Scotland. After a short walk Mary sat on a rock.

"I'll have a rest here, if you don't mind, and stare out to sea. It's a long way across the Atlantic to America, isn't it? A lonely outpost really …"

I thought of the crofters evicted from their land in the infamous Highland Clearances and brought to beaches like this to be herded onto boats and sent across the Atlantic. The Clearances completely changed life in the Highlands and the western isles from the early 18th century. Traditional crofters (subsistence farmers) had their land confiscated and their houses destroyed to make way for the more lucrative endeavour of sheep farming by entitled (often absentee) landowners or lowlanders from the south of Scotland, many aligned to English society and culture. But opportunistic Highlanders looking to increase their farmland were also behind this movement and many crofters were slaughtered in the process. It led to the systematic depopulation of these regions and the dispersal of clan chiefs.

One catalyst for the Clearances was the series of Jacobite rebellions led by Charles Edward Stuart (Bonnie Prince Charlie), seeking to return the House of Stuart to the British throne. This culminated in the ferocious Battle of Culloden, near Inverness, in 1746, in which the Scots Jacobites were brutally defeated by the English army. With English government forces now in control in Scotland, Scottish/Gaelic culture was dismantled. While it sounds bizarre today, the government also banned the wearing of tartan, as well as bagpipe music and any adherence to old clan customs.

The Clearances led to a catastrophic number of deaths and are now classed by many historians as acts of genocide

on the Scottish people, which is why much of the Highlands and islands today still carries the heavy weight of its
history – and nowhere more so than the region of
Sutherland, where we were heading the next day.

While we lingered on the beach, I had other things on
my mind, particularly the Iron Age. I wandered along the
bank of sand topped with grass, raking it with a long stick,
searching for the edge of a cist, which was over-optimistic
really. But I was delighted, after a 10-minute walk, to find
a jumble of bones at the back of the beach. Long bones I
couldn't identify, maybe leg bones. My imagination was
flying. I poked them about on the sand and took some
photos. No signs of a solid cist, though, or Iron Age
trinkets either. The area probably needed a good dig
around with a shovel.

I went back to where Mary was sitting on her rock, still
staring out to sea, as if she'd never seen an ocean before.

"I found some long bones up the beach," I told her,
breaking her reverie.

Her hazel eyes went big. "Not the Iron Age stuff?"

"That would be jammy, eh? Finding bones on our first
visit here."

"There are better souvenirs to take home than tibias
and fibias," she scoffed.

I laughed. She always delighted me with her squinty
take on life.

"Let's go back and tell Ted."

Back at the guesthouse, Ted rubbed his chin when I
told him about my find.

"Long bones, you say. Hmm, could be cow bones. All
sorts of things get washed up on the shore in storms. I'll
go there myself and take a look."

We left before Ted went to the beach, and headed for
Harris, taking the southern road and passing through

moorland dotted with inland lochs to Carloway, at the head of Loch Roag. The settlement has one of the best preserved Iron Age brochs (hollow stone-walled structures) in Scotland, perched on a craggy peak of rock.

I parked the car near the inlet for a walk down to the water and found a middle-aged guy sitting on a grassy bank staring out across the water, sparkling under a blast of sudden spring sunshine. He looked to be a farmer or labourer of some kind, wearing a blue boiler suit and a grey woollen beanie. He seemed so at peace with himself and I wanted to take his picture, but not from afar, so I approached him and asked if he would mind, pointing to my camera.

He looked rather terrified, or just intensely shy perhaps, and spoke first in Gaelic and then in soft English. I took a quick photo and then felt guilty for ruining his peaceful moment and told him so. I got a thin smile but before I could engage him in any more chat, he got up and bounded away like a frightened antelope. I couldn't blame him really. In the early 1990s, few people visited Harris and Lewis, apart from mainland Scots, which made it a very special place back then. Now it has become a popular haunt for others trying to escape the over-development of mainland Britain, and its stresses.

The road to Harris cuts across central Lewis, passing through moody moorland, with a view of lochs and hills. Harris lies across a narrow isthmus. I had planned a visit to Luskentyre, on the west coast, described as one of the most beautiful white-sand beaches in Europe. We didn't make it there because it was harder to reach than expected, but nearby Seilebost beach was just as spectacular with its long stretch of white sand. Photos of the beach in high summer show a dazzling, pale blue sea that I would have found irresistible for swimming, icy cold or not.

Several hours later, after driving around most of Harris, I stopped at a post office/shop on the edge of a village to send a letter. It was as eccentric as any shop I'd seen on Scottish islands. On the counter was the usual slew of tourist tat, shortbread tins, and comical postcards of sheep in wellies standing under umbrellas. The postmistress here did everything in the shop. She was dressed in a thick Harris tweed skirt and a big orange sweater, with a tartan scarf wound round her neck, all in clashing colours.

Behind the counter were shelves crammed with an array of disparate items, so if you needed a tin of soup and a pair of secateurs, this would be the go-to place. A box of veg sat on the lower shelf, with one dispirited lettuce that should probably have had an armed guard looking after it. I imagined there wouldn't be another one for quite a few miles. At the far end of the shelves on hangers were woollen jumpers and cardigans, knitted locally, the woman told me, using natural dyes extracted from island plants and gorses, which would account for their wonderful earthy colours. I bought one on a whim, a slouchy, slightly too big, green jumper with black trim.

The label said Jeanie Moss Creations, which piqued my imagination and I fantasised that Jeanie was a struggling but industrious local, knitting her heart out day and night in front of a peat fire in a kind of blackhouse atmosphere, keeping up her energy with a box of Tunnock's tea cakes. As it turned out, it was one of the best jumpers I'd ever bought, warm like a fisherman's pullover and scented, I fancied, with Hebridean magic. I kept that jumper for years, and still have it, and every time I wear it, I'm right back there, in the post office on Harris, a place that doesn't feel at all like it's at the end of the world. It feels like it's on a planet of its own. And long may that continue.

When I got back to the car, I pulled out my purchase. Mary gave me a sardonic look.

"There was I thinking you only liked designer knitwear," she said.

"It is. Look. Jeanie Moss Creations."

She snorted with laughter as we drove off.

Most ordinary Scots don't take to any kind of pretension and that's one of the things I love about my own race. If you get above yourself, get too 'pan loafy', you'll be brought down straight away, usually with a sarcastic comment, that the Scots excel at, not least my own family. In Australia, there's a similar attitude. And a syndrome to go with it called the Tall Poppy Syndrome where, if you start getting too full of yourself, you'll be scythed down in moments. I feel certain the syndrome has its provenance with the Scots who first went to Australia, no doubt occasionally as convicts.

After another long day of driving we returned to the guest house and were met by Ted.

"I saw the bones. Definitely cow, I'd say. I had a dig about with a shovel too but didn't find any cists. I mean, they don't pop out all the time."

"Thanks be for that," Mary said, with a curdled expression on her face as she trooped off to refresh herself for an early dinner.

We left Lewis the next day, setting sail for the mainland across the Minch, with its Blue Mermen threatening to commit a watery felony amid the white caps in the middle of the channel.

As I watched the island fade into a Hebridean mist, I felt sad to be leaving what I felt was a truly unique place, a quiet place. It moved to its own beat: its remoteness and its strict religious observance seemed to have cut it off from most of the materialism and mayhem of the rest of the world. However, round its edges it bore the incongruity I've often found on Scottish islands and remote coastal outposts: a shiver of melancholy offset by amusing eccentricity, which seems to make life strangely bearable in these cold, far-flung places, and magical too. You just couldn't replicate it anywhere else but here.

* * * * *

Sutherland was as beautiful and as remote as I'd expected it would be. It's one of the most dramatic regions of Scotland, with some of its highest, rugged mountains, and white-sand beaches. The landscape is vast and raw, with miles of moorland, bogs, lochs and scores of lochans (small lochs).

It is dominated by its spectacular mountains like Bheinn Mhor and the famous Suilven, which from certain angles resembles a monolithic helmet of rock. Everywhere the land is pockmarked with the outlines of croft houses, just the walls mostly, lying in the peaty ground like ancient skeletons.

Spectacular as it is, Sutherland for me resonated with the sense of loss I expected to find from its own harsh experience of the Clearances, with waves of evictions in the 19th century, pushed through by the brutal Duke of Sutherland.

He was an English politician and landowner, who banished some 15,000 crofters to the coast and took over their land for sheep farming. The scale of the Clearances here, more than most places, has left a vast swathe of beautiful but empty moorland.

The appropriate song for this leg of the journey was Wolfstone's haunting ballad *The Braes of Sutherland*, written by Ivan Drever, the band's singer/guitarist. The ballad reflects the tragedy of enforced emigration of crofters, and the loss of their native land.

I turned the track up a bit, relishing its moody electric violin accompaniment, and slid a look towards Mary to see how she'd take it. She was humming away, trying to pick out the words – a Celtic Rock fan at last!

We detoured on the way north to Loch Assynt to see Ardveck Castle, just a ruin now with walls and a bit of a tower and once the home of the MacLeod clan. It was said to be the seat of many dark deeds, as the Highlands often were, with their clan rivalries and bloodshed on a Sicilian scale. But Ardveck Castle, set beside the loch's rocky shore and surrounded by wild, empty moorland, had a darkly romantic quality about it that so many Scottish castles possess, especially in isolated locations. So compelling was this site, it was tempting to stay longer but we still had a fair bit of road to cover.

After a long drive we finally reached Durness, on the north coast, with its rugged seascape and beaches backed by high jagged cliffs. There was much to see along this coast, such as the strangely named Smoo Cave, with an interior said to resemble a Gothic cathedral. To the west was the famous Cape Wrath, which we had no time to visit. I couldn't imagine dragging my mother there, a place that sounded cold and troublesome.

It was late afternoon. The wind was getting up, howling in from the North Sea, and it felt increasingly bitter. I needed to sort some accommodation for the night. In those days there was very little tourist infrastructure in remote places like Durness, whereas now there are guest houses and cabins, caravan sites and adventure activities galore. On the main road, however, I saw an old two-storey hotel facing the sea and I parked at the front. It had weather-worn stone work and flaking, high sash windows and it looked like it had seen better days, back in the 19th century, no doubt. Its name was unremarkable, painted on a scuffed wooden sign over the front entrance. We decided that given its face-off with the North Sea, it should be called Storm Pile – and that's how we referred to it from then on.

The front door was unlocked. A bell tinkled when I pushed it open onto a dark hallway with a small reception desk. It was as quiet as a grave. Few visitors would be this far north in early May, and if they stopped at all it would be just for a night, on the way to somewhere else, as we were. There was a dank, unaired smell about the building and it was about as welcome as Hitchcock's Bates Motel. I toyed with the idea of leaving, to find a cosier hostelry, but before I could a stout, middle-aged woman approached the desk. She'd come from a dark room at the end of the corridor, which seemed to be the kitchen, and introduced herself as Mrs McAlister. She was swathed in woollen layers and had a messy up-do, some of which hung in strands around her neck.

She wrinkled her brow when I told her I needed a room, which made me fear there were no vacancies, though the town was hardly thrumming with people. But then, suggestive of a contrary nature, she said, brightly: "Aye, that's fine. I've got a twin-bedded room with the sea view. Will that do?"

"Yes, that would be just terrific," I said, over-inflating my enthusiasm.

The crinkling, troubled brow returned as I filled out a registration form, which spiked my curiosity even more when I discovered we were the only guests and there were around 10 other rooms.

"Your mother's with you, you say?"

"She's in the car."

Mrs McAlister peered through the glass panel of the front door, as if to settle something in her mind, probably about my sanity in hoicking my mother up to this draughty outpost.

"I don't put the heating on till 5.30pm. This place costs a muckle load of money to heat, so I have to ration it. I hope that suits. And I don't do any evening meals. There's a café down the road, called the Mystic Kelpie."

I queried the name with a smile, thinking it sounded like something from the west coast of America, not the perishing north coast of Scotland, though the word kelpie has mythical cred, a Gaelic word meaning water horse.

She frowned. "No ... well, that's its unofficial name, but it's what you'd call a play on the owner's name, Mr Kerpey. Long story, dear, but locals know it as the Mystic Kelpie, which, to be honest, I prefer to Kerpey's Cafe." Oh, too much information there, but it made me smile.

"Anyway, the owner shuts it when there's no-one around and I imagine it will be shut tonight. There's the pub not far from here, where you should be able to get something to eat. Not sure what that might be tonight, though it's not the bonniest place for an evening meal, I admit. And the TV's always blaring," she said, with a grimace.

It struck me that Mrs McAlister was wasted in her profession as hotel owner when she should have been working for the Scottish Tourist Board, with her flare for highlighting the positives of the town's dining facilities, and other assets. Clearly, it was going to be a long night, and my stomach was rumbling already.

I got the bags out of the car and ushered Mary inside, feeling somewhat guilty that this hotel stay would confirm what she'd originally felt about highland roving, that it would be dreich. Storm Pile was certainly cold and I wondered how we'd manage for the next hour or so until 5.30. The two women had a short chat while the key was handed over and we went to our room. It was huge, sparsely furnished, with long sash windows with a view to the sea. The view was glorious at least, the white-capped waves hurtling in from the north.

"It's perishing cold," Mary said, rubbing her hands together. On one chest of drawers there was a kettle and some tea, coffee and biscuits. I quickly made hot drinks and we ate all the biscuits, which had been stacked on a scuffed tin tray with a highland setting. We had some food left over from lunch, a sandwich bought at a tourist shop on the way. We ate that as well.

We still felt chilly and at a loss what to do in those awkward late afternoon hours when it's too late and cold to wander about outside and too early for dinner – if a meal was at all available.

"I'm getting into bed. It'll be warmer at least, till the flamin' central heating goes on," said Mary. She pulled back the eiderdown on one of the twin beds and got in, with her clothes on. What the hell! I did the same, in my own narrow bed. We felt tired as well from a long day. We chattered for a bit, however, like teenagers having an uncomfortable sleepover, somewhere inauspicious.

"You know I do miss that cosy room we had at the guest house on Lewis, and even the doolally bridal suite in Stornoway," she said, pulling the eiderdown up around her chin.

"So do I." And once again I missed the Hebrides and marvelled that such a wild, treeless, remote place could actually seem cosy. Then we both fell into a dead sleep and woke up as the radiators came to life with a banging and clunking, like the engine room on an old ship. However, the temperature remained cold for a while as we lay in our beds, watching the light starting to fade outside. I was reminded, not for the first time in my life, that the biggest obstacle in Scottish dwellings, even with central heating sometimes, was the cold. It's a particular kind of cold that gets right into your bones.

My father had lived as a child in a tenement block in the Calton, in the deprived east end of Glasgow. He was born into an Irish family and most of the seven kids had slept in one double bed, top to tail, covered in a multitude of blankets and winter coats. The cold is what he remembered most about his early life, amid all the other deprivations.

I wondered if my mother was thinking right this minute of the snug house she'd left in Sydney, with a toasty sun beating down on it.

I got out of bed at last at six, lured by thoughts of organising dinner.

"Look, while you freshen up, I'll slip out and check the café and the pub Mrs McAlister talked about, and see what they're like. But I don't hold out much hope."

I quickly tidied myself so I didn't look like I'd just crept out of bed, put on a thick coat and sloped out the front door. An arc of sea spray was sailing over the road as the high tide reached the back of the beach.

The Mystic Kelpie was shut and Mr Kerpey was nowhere to be seen. The trouble was, so early in the season, nothing would be properly open. The pub had a TV blaring, right enough, showing a football match, and the bar was smoky and unappealing.

I asked about food and was told dinner was off because the chef had come down with a cold, but they could make us a sandwich. I trailed back to the hotel with a heavy heart.

Mary was combing her wavy hair and applying lipstick at an ancient mirror.

"Do you fancy sandwiches for tea," I asked her.

"You're joking, right?"

"Wish I was. What if I have a chat with the owner and see if I can twist her arm a bit and appeal to her sense of hospitality?"

"Good luck with that," said Mary, with a wink.

I walked down to the kitchen, where Mrs McAlister seemed to spend all her time. It was the warmest room in the building. She was sitting at a square wooden table near the oven, reading a women's magazine. She looked up quizzically. I explained my futile search for dinner and then asked her if she could possibly whip us up a simple meal, an omelette or something warm on toast. She pulled a bit of a face. Time to invent a simple story.

"My mother's not feeling up to par today. Cold and tired from the journey up from Ullapool." I gave her a look of quiet appeal. She sat a moment, staring at her magazine.

"Och, well, I've got a pot of soup on the go. It's just tatties and a wee bit of carrot. Nothing special, but you're both welcome to come down for a bowl. Can't have guests starving to death, can I?"

"No, probably not," I said, sweetly, as I turned to go back to the room to collect my mother.

Mrs McAlister had set three places at the wooden table and put a plate of white bread slices in the middle, with a wedge of butter on a glass dish. She ladled soup into the bowls and put them on the table. Mary shot me a jaded look when hers was delivered. The soup had a thin grey sheen about it and I hoped it tasted better than it looked. But as I'd expected, it tasted of nothing much at all but boiled potatoes, and I guessed our host had watered it down after I made my appeal for dinner. She apologised for not having much else to eat but assured us we'd find a nice hot breakfast in the dining room tomorrow. *If we survive the night,* I thought. I even thought of asking her if we could just have the breakfast now but imagined she'd girn quite a bit over that idea.

"I don't do dinner this early in the year, you see. It's impossible to tell who will drive by, as you did, and just come in for a last-minute booking."

"That's all right, Mrs McAlister. We understand how things are in the tourism industry here," said Mary, sounding like a seasoned traveller but with a sardonic edge to her voice that made me smile.

"Call me Sheena, dear," she said, offering us both another ladleful of thin soup.

We battled on with it, hardly talking at all, and I had the grim notion that this soup had probably been on the go for some time. It was, after all, a Scottish custom for ordinary folk to have a pot of something bubbling on the back burner, especially in winter. I painfully remembered a story from a delightful old book dated 1836 called *Traditions of Perth* by George Penny. It said the 'labouring classes' for their dinner often ate 'water kail', green curly kail in a soup with other seasonal vegetables. During that time in Perth, a popular joke had done the rounds that when anything seemed old it was described 'as auld as Muirton kail'.

It relates to the case of a miserly farmer from the area of Muirton in Perth, who instructed his cook to add the remains of one day's water kail into the next day's batch with additional veg or meat scraps. This dubious mix eventually laid one his servants very low indeed, with the result it was the subject of a local court case. It was established that the offending soup, having been added to each day, had in fact become seven years old, and no surprise that it had turned into a great festering brew. The judge condemned the soup to be thrown into the sewer. I hoped Sheena's soup hadn't been going that long, but who would know? It looked pretty dead to me. All the same, it was hot and the bread was filling – and we'd hopefully live to travel another day.

After dinner, Sheena lit up a cigarette and offered us a whisky, which was very welcome in the circumstances, though I imagine soup and whisky aren't ideal pairings. It revived us at least.

"So, it's Perth you come from originally, isn't it, my dears? But what in God's name made you want to come here on holiday from sunny Australia – in May? I mean, June and July can be bonnie, excepting the scourge of the midges, but May. Och, as we say, 'Ne'r cast a cloot till May's oot'." It means don't put your winter clothes away in May because it's likely to be cold enough to freeze your arse off, or something like that.

I saw the corner of Mary's mouth twitch at Sheena's slight condescension.

"We wanted to see the Highlands, something different from the usual trips back to Perth that we generally do, you know," I explained.

Sheena shook her head and stared at us through a cloud of exhaled smoke. She knew nothing, of course, of visitors varying their travel itineraries for unaccountable reasons, only that occasionally folk washed up in Durness. At least Mary now had a warm glow about her face after a few more sips of the whisky soother.

"Well, do you know something, Sheena? We've been out to Harris and Lewis. Not many can say that, can they? My daughter's idea," she said with a proprietorial lift of her chin. "Amazing place it is. Had no idea the islands were like that. It was awfie quiet and bonnie." She fluttered her eyes in my direction to see how I liked her glowing endorsement of the trip. I did, very much.

"Really! All the way over there? Well, I've not been to the Hebrides and it's not likely either. I'm lucky if I ever get down to Inverness," said Sheena, puffing on her cigarette.

As we lay in our twin beds that night, talking over the day, the covers and coats layered on top of us in Glasgow tenement style, because the heating was now off, if it was ever properly on, I asked my mother if she'd really meant what she said to Sheena about the Hebrides.

"Aye, I did," she said firmly, levering herself onto one elbow. "I know I girned about sea crossings and all that, but I'm grateful in the end you took me to the islands. I really am. I've seen something special I'd never have seen on my own. And I tell you, I'm missing Shirley's fine cooking now and the cosy room, as I told you before. Not the reeking blackhouse though. I draw the line at that," she said, chortling softly.

Maybe it was the cold, or some residual hunger, or the sound of the fractious sea pelting the shore, but I felt my eyes well up a bit and I was grateful it was too dark for my mother to see it.

"Well, I'm glad, Mum, really I am," I said in a small voice. And I was, and relieved that she'd got something out of the trip. It was no isolated endorsement either, because to everyone we met after that who happened to ask about our Scottish jaunt, she raved about the Hebrides.

One of her unknowable layers seemed to have suddenly peeled away. I started to think we could have taken on more islands, bigger adventures, and we would, if there was a next time.

The following morning, after real food at last, the fortifying fry-up we'd been promised, we continued on our way. John O' Groats, in Caithness, is the most northerly point of the British mainland, with its famous white signpost telling you, should you need reminding, that Land's End (Cornwall), New York and several other disparate places are miles and miles away.

There wasn't much at John O' Groats but a small harbour, though the Castle of Mey, once the home of the Queen Mother, was in the area and some of the cliffs with tall sea stacks were said to be astonishing. We motored down the east coast road to Inverness, stopping along the way at a coastal hotel that was pleasant but short on real comfort. We arrived in Inverness late in the afternoon and managed to catch the tourist office before it closed. I asked about the best hotels in the town and booked one for two nights. After the dreary experience of Durness, we needed to treat ourselves, and I felt guilty that my mother had put up with a few discomforts along the way. We ate well and slept well, drank cocktails at the bar before dinner and chortled over our trip so far.

On the day we left Inverness, I decided to visit the nearby battlefield of Culloden because of its significant role in Scotland's history, particularly the Jacobite uprisings. It was here that Bonnie Prince Charlie was defeated by the English in his bid to put the Stuarts back on the British throne, and he eventually fled from Scotland to France. It was to become the last major battle fought on British soil.

While the day had started off a bit cold, it was now much greyer, with nary a hint of spring in the landscape. I left Mary in the car, as I knew she wouldn't want to traipse around the battlefield on Drumossie Moor, and went off to explore it on my own.

The moor had a chilling aura. It was a forsaken kind of place, vast, flat, with sodden ground covered in gorse and wintery-thin trees. On the day of the battle, April 16, 1746, the 5,000 Jacobites, mostly Highlanders, in just 40 minutes of savage battle were outnumbered and defeated by the English army of 9,000 troops, led by the Duke of Cumberland. Some 1,000 Scots died and were buried on the moor. Stone grave markers commemorate some of the clan groups buried thereabouts, including Fraser, MacGillivray, MacDonald and Maclean, though each site is said to have included other unrecorded clans as well. In short, they were all mass graves.

A tall stone cairn in the middle of the battlefield, however, offers more of a rousing sight in this gruesome place and mentions "the graves of the gallant Highlanders who fought for Scotland and Prince Charlie ..."

I made my way out of the moor, proud of the poor souls who perished here, but I was glad to be leaving. Although I was well wrapped up with a hat and scarf, before I'd even got back to the car an hour later I felt I was suddenly coming down with a cold. There was something that was still ailing about the battlefield. I'd felt it strongly - the Curse of Culloden perhaps. Even Mary remarked I looked "a wee bit peely wally". Pale and uninteresting! She spoke too soon because by the time we arrived in Perth a few days later, she'd also come down with the cold, which was unfortunate after the pampering we'd had in Inverness.

We planned to stay at the Kinnoull Guest House, a small four-star hotel on the posh side of the river Tay, for four nights. I thought that would be enough time to shake off the colds and still be able to catch up with one or two relatives, part of the ritual for my mother of going back 'home', while I had other things in mind. I'd stayed at the Kinnoull a few years previously, drawn to its location beneath the famous hill of the same name, with its woodland walks and an old tower on an escarpment overlooking the Tay river. I had found the guest house comfortable and the owners, the Farquarsons, to be efficient, if slightly stitched-up. What could go wrong? Well, two years or so in the hospitality trade is a long time.

Once we'd checked in, I discovered the Farquarsons had become even more pernickety than I remembered, with a slew of house rules and suggestions for visitors. The wife gave us a river-facing room for our stay, which was slightly more expensive, and she was unimpressed with our increasing sniffing and sneezing and remarked on it with a churlish comment, as if arriving at a hotel feeling under the weather was tantamount to committing a felony. She dropped the room key in the palm of my hand.

"I hope you'll get better soon."

The room was pleasant, with twin beds and a TV opposite and a nice ensuite bathroom. The view was glorious, overlooking the edge of the city on the Tay, and the Grampian mountains way in the distance.

After a sturdy breakfast the next day, we planned to drive into town and do the expected things: shop in the High Street, or walk by the famous peaty-coloured Tay river, famous for its salmon fishing. But as we got ready to go out, we both felt poorly and decided to rest for a couple of hours in the room to shake off the cold. When a maid knocked on the door to offer a quick tidy-up and change of towels, I told her we didn't need anything because I couldn't be bothered with all the faff of room maintenance, a circumstance that unfortunately brought Mrs Farquarson swiftly to the door.

"No fresh towels?" she whined, peering past my head to see what exactly we were doing in the room in the middle of the morning. The rules indicated rooms were supposed to be vacated by 10.30 to allow for cleaning.

"We're still not well with these colds," I sniffed. She peered again, sternly, around my head. *Rude woman*, I thought.

"Would you mind leaving us, please. We don't need anything right now."

She pulled a face and I politely shut the door. Mary was on the bed, propped up on a pillow, reading a psychological thriller and drinking tea.

"Jeez. So many rules here."

She rolled her eyes. "I could have told you that. This is the posh side of Perth. If you live on this side, you're going to be pan loafy and picky. Always was like that."

By lunchtime, even though we weren't feeling a lot better, we decided to go out just to escape the owner's attentions. The fresh air would do us good, I reckoned.

I was sitting at the desk by the window, a piece of newspaper on the glass top, trying to polish a pair of black leather boots. The spongy applicator tip had hardened and while I was zealously squeezing the tip hard onto one of the boots to release some polish, suddenly a great spurt came out. It landed on the boot and flustered me, causing me to drop the applicator on the floor. As with all these kinds of mishaps, like dropping your toast jam-side down, the applicator landed on the spongy end, depositing a small black patch onto the beige carpet, fairly new, by the look of it.

"Oh, shit!" I yelped. "Boot polish on the carpet!"

Mary was sitting on the end of the bed, ready to go out. She peered down at the black spot, with a lemony pucker of lips.

"Oh, Mrs F won't like that. Your coat's on a shoogly peg now, pet!"

I laughed at her take on the Scots expression, meaning 'you're in deep trouble now', though it usually means, 'you're fired'. But nothing else right then was worth a laugh.

"You should have been more careful," she added.

"Now don't start! I *was* careful, but didn't plan to drop the whole thing on the floor. Oh, Jeez!" I said, my runny nose beginning to drip as well.

I dashed to the toilet to blow my nose and fetched my make-up remover with the idea it might help remove the stain. I rubbed it in with a damp facecloth and blotted it with toilet paper as much as I could, but it only seemed to make matters worse. Mary was standing over me now, hands on hips, the default maternal position for disapproval.

I tried to ignore her gimlet eyes on my cleaning manoeuvre, in case we ended up in an argy-bargy in our tetchy, cold-ridden state, which would draw the staff to our door.

"I think you need some carpet cleaner," she said, turning around and sitting on the bed again.

"Yes, good idea. I'll go out right away to get some."

I covered the stain quickly with one of my slippers and got my coat and bag.

"So, don't let anyone into the room while I'm gone. And don't go touching the stain, okay?"

"Okay, okay. I'm on the case," she said, unwrapping a shortbread biscuit from the tea tray.

"And don't get crumbs everywhere."

"I don't think crumbs are the issue here any more," she said, her eyes flickering to the one slipper on the carpet, possibly a dire giveaway of a furnishing mishap. Two would have been smarter, but I was in a hurry.

I dashed out and drove over Perth's famous old bridge, forgetting how much I loved seeing it every time I came back here, its pink stone arches and the fast peaty current broiling underneath. But at that moment I had carpets on my mind. I parked near the High Street and dashed into a hardware shop, where I bought what looked like the easiest, fool-proof cleaner, except that it came in a long metal spray can that I then had to carry into the hotel hidden in a plastic bag, obviously. But because of the length of the can, it looked very much like I was smuggling in booze and I felt my hands tremble when I got to the front door and saw Mrs Farquarson hovering about like a heat-seeking missile. She eyed up the bag.

"Everything all right with you both up there?" she said, her brows knitting together with worry. "You look at lot better though. Do you want us to tidy up the room a bit for you?"

"Not right now, thanks," I said, firmly.

I ran up the stairs, shaking my head at this obsessive cleaning syndrome the woman was afflicted with. Mary was still sitting on the bed, staring at the offending patch on the carpet, like a dog guarding its food bowl. I set to work on the stain, fizzing it with the cleaner. It had to be left for 10 minutes, in which time, of course, the owner tapped at the door and again I managed to persuade her that all was well.

"Has Scotland always had a thing about rules?" I asked Mary after I'd swiftly shut the door.

"We're proud people, you know that. We don't like anyone to think we're poor, or common, or daft. That's all. When I was a kid my mother would say, 'Don't go out with that long face. You don't want people to think you're not happy'."

"But not being happy, Jeez, it's not a crime. No-one's happy all the time. What did Granny imagine people would think? That her kids were all working secretly down a coal mine?"

"I don't know. She just didn't like a long face dragging along beside her."

I laughed. You had to really. I fetched the damp facecloth and started to rub at the frothy stain, like Lady

Macbeth covering up after murdering discount carpeting. In the end, by rubbing and blotting it with loo paper, and working up a sweat, the stain was more or less out and only someone with a strange, obsessive mind would detect a misdemeanour here – someone like Mrs F.

We went out that afternoon for a drive just beyond the outskirts of Perth, rather than a city walk. We headed north, past the famous Meikleour Hedge, the tallest hedge in the world, standing 100ft high and almost 600 yards long. It was planted in 1746, the same year as the Battle of Culloden, which was thoroughly fixed in my mind now. Every time I'm in Perth I always put the great hedge on my itinerary. Daft really, but as long as it's there and some ned hasn't gone mad with a pair of hedge trimmers and demolished it, then I feel all's right with Scotland.

We left our city exploits for the next day, when we were both feeling a lot better. In the afternoon, Mary was to meet up with some of her old acquaintances while I indulged in retail therapy and a few hours in the art gallery.

On our last full day, we set out for the wide, grassy North Inch, one of the main city parks, which borders the river close to the old Perth bridge. While the bridge was built in 1771 by John Smeaton, there had been several previous structures, some washed away during floods, with the earliest crossing recorded in the 13th century. But it was the Georgian terrace at the back of the park we'd really come to see, my parents' first address after they married and my first home as a newborn baby. Ironically, while we had come back separately over the years to this address for a sentimental visit, we'd never come back together, until now.

Rose Terrace in its time was said to have been one of the best Georgian streets in Scotland, dating from around 1800. Perth was once the nation's capital and the early kings held court here. In a curious local story, I discovered the freedom fighter William Wallace (the Braveheart) was said to have carried out a romantic tryst near Rose Terrace after he fell for an attractive young maid. In order to slip through the city gates and avoid his enemies, he dressed as a priest. Later, when he was ready to sneak out of the city again, he dressed as a woman, having borrowed some of his paramour's clothing, showing us that there was more to the macho, blue-faced warrior image than we hitherto thought.

Perth became an important trading port in the Middle Ages and city centre still maintains its original medieval grid pattern, though the original city walls are almost gone. In the 1950s, Rose Terrace might have seemed an illustrious address for a young couple starting out, though their finances extended only to renting a basement flat and not one of the finer residences above. The flat had been cold, damp and unhealthy due to the number of times in the city's history the river Tay had burst its banks and flooded the Inch, as well as the nearby terraces.

We stood on the pavement, looking down at the basement of the terraced house where we'd lived. The front flat below had now been turned into a children's nursery. Mary shook her head.

"I wonder that they'd put kids down there. It was awfie dreich and damp when we lived there, and especially for you as a baby. It's probably near as bad today." We had moved out of the flat after a year or so, rehomed in a small council house on the edge of the countryside, with a view towards Scone Palace, which had been a remarkable bonus.

Beyond an iron gate and a set of deep mossy steps was an open door leading to the close. The close is a feature of old Scottish terraces and tenement blocks, a passageway that connects the front to the back of the building and contains the front doors of the lower dwellings. We walked into the close, drawn by a patch of sunlight from the back garden.

Mary stopped at the scuffed green door of our old home at the back of the building. She put her palm out and silently held it against the door for a few moments. It was a curious, almost affectionate gesture, as if she were trying to channel the past.

I stood quietly and watched her, wondering what was going through her mind, even though I was sure it was my father, John, she would be thinking about. After a few moments she moved her hand, whispering something I couldn't quite catch, and turned towards the garden. It was lit with sudden spring sunshine, with daffodils sprouting vibrantly in overgrown corners. There was a lawn of sorts and a few garden sheds. We sat on a low stone wall, facing the rear of the building, with the sun on our backs. The place also made me feel oddly nostalgic, for a life I couldn't remember as a baby.

"I suppose you weren't that sorry to leave here. I can just imagine how cold it must have been in winter," I said.

"No, I wasn't, but there are lovely memories here all the same, being newly married, you arriving, and the war well behind us. It was a good enough life in many ways. When we emigrated to Australia it should have been a dream move to a life in the sun. It was, but it was also harder than we imagined."

"Is that why you cried regularly when we first got to Australia, because you missed Perth, your mother, and especially those Scottish bacon rolls, remember?" I said, laughing softly to lighten the mood because I felt we were slipping into melancholy.

"I remember all that, yes. And the tears, but it was a culture shock at first. When we signed up for the assisted passage scheme at Australia House in London, no-one told you how hard it was going to be. What you'd be giving up. And there were plenty of promises about jobs and houses that were never kept. Migrants had to stay for two years in Australia, or otherwise repay the normal cost of the return fare, instead of the 10 quid for each adult. Some Brits had a terrible time settling in. They hated it; paid back their fares and went home."

'Ten Pound Poms', that's what we'd been, like refugees in our own way, sent on the long, six-week sea voyage on ships that were near the end of their working lives. Around 1.5 million Britons were lured to Australia from World War Two until the 1970s for a new life, and for Australia it was part of its 'populate or perish' initiative to grow the country.

On the ship, we were separated into men- and women-only cabins, with young children staying with their mothers. And cabins were also shared with other families. It was a set-up that strained many new marriages, though my mother confessed there was nightly canoodling in all the lifeboats that hung just over the edge of the decks "if you were lucky enough to find one empty", she said with a wink.

"Was it all worth it in the end? I mean, despite the hardships, plenty of struggling Scots migrated in the 1950s and 60s, and most have lived happy lives."

She didn't answer straight off. I could sense her mind churning back in time.

"I think it was worth it. We took a chance, gave up everything and went. It took me a while to love Australia, and I do now. I love the weather anyway."

I knew my father loved Australia. During the war years he'd survived one of the worst battles in Europe, on the front line at Monte Cassino in Italy, 1944. In the beginning, he said the war had been a chance to leave behind the poverty of a childhood spent in the notorious east end of Glasgow. It brought adventure, excitement at times, but also some of the worst war experiences imaginable, which he never liked to talk about. Australia, for him, had a different narrative. It was the ultimate escape. He deserved that at least, and while he lived there he enjoyed his dream life in the sun.

We lapsed into a thoughtful silence. My attention was captured by the back sash window of the flat, and I recalled one of our old family photographs: the window completely up and my mother sitting on the sill in a summer dress, her legs dangling out and me on her lap, both smiling and soaking up some proper sun. It reminded me that life in the basement was also sweet at times.

"The thing about leaving Scotland, well … sometimes you have to move far away, to change course, you know," she said.

"To change your destiny, you mean?"

"Yes, I suppose you could say that. Otherwise, when you're poor, how else do you get to step up a bit." There was a little catch in her voice. I knew what she meant, even if some of our family, who'd stayed behind, wouldn't have got it at all.

In my own experiences of returning to Perth, I had spoken with people who hadn't chosen the migrant route from hardship, but who told me they thought it was *them* who had been the pioneers, the tough ones who persisted in their homeland while others, like us, 'ran away', turning our backs on our heritage.

There might be some truth in that, but having seen the decaying croft houses of the Highlands and the Hebrides, abandoned because their residents had been violently driven out during the Clearances, or through famine, I couldn't imagine that, by comparison, staying behind in Perth in post-war years was any kind of endurance trial. Perhaps the remainers were just less adventurous, and their resentment of our easier lifestyle overseas was often palpable.

But at that moment, sitting in the backyard of an old Georgian building in the spring sunshine, I couldn't be sure that any of that really mattered, one way or another. But Mary was still mulling something over.

"What about you?" she asked. "Are you glad we went to Australia? Because I know how sentimental you get sometimes about Scotland. I've seen it on this trip at times. And there's a restlessness in you."

"Yes and no," I answered vaguely.

I was restless, I couldn't deny that. It was hard not to be when you have to go as a child to the other end of the planet, to a different way of life, when you haven't come to grips properly with the first one.

Australia, for a child, however, turned out to be pretty good: endless sunshine, surf beaches, mangos all year round. But here's the thing: once I left high school, I left Australia. I went on a kind of gap year, to Scotland for a few weeks and then to Greece for a year and back to the UK, to England, where I took a degree course. I didn't return to Australia again for 10 years.

Throughout my peripatetic life, despite the fact that the many other locations I've visited as a journalist, or privately, have thrilled me, the link with Scotland has never been broken. I think I knew that for sure on this particular trip. Like my mother, resting a hand on that scuffed green door in the close, I've had my hand resting lightly on Scotland all my days, trying to fathom my place in it. And at that point I still hadn't achieved it.

"Would you ever want to come back here to live?" I asked her.

"What? At my age, in my seventies? You must be joking! But would you … want to come back?" she asked, with a slightly panicked look in her lovely hazel eyes.

"I don't think so … no."

That's what I thought at that particular moment, and what I knew she'd want to hear. But I wasn't sure it was the whole truth.

She nodded, as if satisfied with the response. We left the old place, walking slowly back along Rose Terrace to the car, arm in arm, quietly happy, as if we'd laid a few ghosts to rest.

When we finally left Perth, on our way south to Edinburgh for a few days before flying back to Sydney, we were sorry to be leaving the city itself, but not sorry to be breaking free from OCS, Obsessive Cleaning Syndrome, at the Kinnoull establishment.

At the reception desk, while I paid, Mrs F asked if we'd had a nice stay, and were we feeling better at last.

"Yes, yes, thank you," I said.

Without looking at me, she scribbled out a receipt, and said: "By the way, the stain on the carpet will have to be sorted. I see you had a good go at it. I found your carpet cleaner can in one of the bins at the side of the building."

My eyes were saucer-wide. "Sorry, I don't think I know what you're talking about," I mumbled. I glanced over at Mary. Her face was pink, but not with hilarity – not yet anyway.

"Oh, I think you do," said Mrs F, wagging a finger at me. "I knew something was amiss in your room, all that 'no-room-service' palaver. I feel these things in my bones, you see. It was just a case of finding out what you'd been up to."

I was gobsmacked by her insolence, not to mention her perspicacity with furnishing dramas, and shocked by the severity of her OCS. I assumed we were about to be financially penalised, but she waved us on, like pesky flies.

"Honestly, guests get up to some mischief at times, and there's very little that goes by me, I can assure you. Enjoy your day," she said, then looked away quickly, sorting files on the desk, dusting them with the flat of her hand, completely in character.

Mary managed to get all the way to the front door before bursting into a fit of giggles, which started me off as well, naturally. We laughed all the way to the car.

"Cheeky besom!" she said, glancing towards the building, wiping tears of mirth from her eyes. "Did the room have a hidden camera, do you think?" More giggles.

That bizarre thought nagged at me all the way out of town, until the sight of green rolling hills on the outskirts of Perth and the start of vibrant electric bagpipes on the car's sound system dispelled it.

* * * * *

Despite telling my mother I didn't think I would move back to Scotland, that's exactly what I did, four years later. I went back *with* my mother (another great leap of destiny for her) and a fellow journalist, an endearing Englishman with a Scottish surname, whom I'd met shortly after my return to Australia from the Hebridean trip. Jim would later become my husband and we would share many grand adventures together. We would buy a Victorian house in a Scottish village, warm and roomy enough for Mary too and a restless Jack Russell terrier called Wallace.

While I had given up my role as a feature writer in Sydney, a job that had taken me around the world and allowed me to meet some memorable people, I knew that fascinating interviewees and great adventures lay ahead in Scotland. The country had secured devolution in 1998, with its own Parliament meeting for the first time the following year, promising a more vibrant and optimistic future.

"It's because of that trip we made to Scotland, isn't it?" my mother once said, not long after we'd settled in our village, near Stirling. "I suspected you had something like this skittering in your mind."

I don't know if that was strictly true, and if the seeds of this seismic move were sown on that particular trip. If they were, it was probably at the old Rose Terrace house, where we'd rummaged back into the past and where I might have allowed the notion to fly out that I could complete a certain circle, going back to the beginning of my life. Of course, not every circle, however malformed it may be, needs to be completed, but just sometimes it's too enticing not to make it happen. Even my mother embraced that in the end.

For me, perhaps the expedition back to the homeland was also a continuation of the restlessness I'd had since that first childhood migration, and an attempt to put down roots finally, or just to belong somewhere.

However, a well-travelled writer, with whom I'd once discussed the thorny issue of uprooting and resettling, confessed that "once you're an adult you stop putting down new roots, even in familiar soil". Or perhaps roots become shallower things, easily pulled up without too much damage.

Time would tell.

Chapter 5
There's something about Skye
(Inner Hebrides, Scotland)

IN THE middle of the night in the croft house, we were woken by a frenzied scratching noise in the bedroom.

"What the hell is that?" said Jim. "Sounds like a massive rat!"

We were wide awake now, lying in a traditional Scottish box bed, the kind that's raised off the floor, with a small set of wooden steps at the front. The frantic scratching continued and the sound of nails sliding repeatedly off polished wood as something tried to make its way up the steps, sometimes falling backwards and then starting over again. As this was a box bed, there was no side table nearby to hold a lamp. We just had to lie in the dark and wait.

"It's probably just Wallace," I said in a thin voice, pulling the duvet defensively up to my chin.

"That's not Wallace. He's asleep in his dog bed, surely?"

"Not any more he's not," I said as the scratching finally reached the top step and something bounced onto the bed beside me, with its signature odour of warm fur, slightly musky.

Jim sighed with frustration. "What's got into him?"

"Don't know," I said, as Wallace's questing terrier nature came to the fore, raking back the corner of the duvet, burrowing his way into the bed and settling under my outstretched arm.

"He can't stay, there's hardly room up here for the two us, let alone Wallace as well," Jim complained.

"Well, something has totally freaked him out," I replied, stroking Wallace's furry head. "We'll leave him here for a bit till he calms down."

"I knew the box bed was a bad idea," said Jim, wriggling about, banging his elbow on the wall beside him.

This kind of bed was a practical choice in Scotland in previous centuries, usually made with a solid wooden base and set into a deep wall recess close to the kitchen for warmth. Now it was an acquired taste, even this one, built a few years earlier by the homeowner's husband, with an exquisite carved wooden canopy above, wooden posts and base, into which the mattress fitted snugly. As double beds go, however, it was quite small, for Jim at least. The box bed was fitted longways into the end of the room and Jim was sleeping against the wall. After a couple of nights, he claimed it was too claustrophobic.

"I had nightmares earlier on. I dreamt I was locked in a big box like a coffin and couldn't get out. This bed doesn't agree with me, or maybe it's this room, so I'm not surprised Wallace is going doolally."

"I think the bed's really cosy. And Wallace seems to like it fine. No, it's something else," I said.

But what exactly, I had no idea. Wallace had many terrier faults but he was never usually a restless sleeper. Once he was in his dog bed, he tended to stay there and we'd placed it near the bottom of the stairs when we went to bed, so he'd be nearby. It was usually the case that Wallace spooked more in daylight hours.

He was an adorable young Parson Russell terrier, very handsome with black and white markings, long legs and huge dark eyes, which he used to great effect whenever he wanted something. But he also had madness stitched into his genes, as his Edinburgh breeder had intimated the first time we set eyes on him. Hyperactive and stubborn, early on I had christened him the Pinball With Fur, due to his ability to sprint about our Scottish home for hours without flagging. His stamina was breathtaking. But things did rattle him. Odd things, like doorbells, loose crockery, noisy characters on TV, vacuum cleaners, anything really, or anyone who looked odd to his terrier sensibilities – and there were many of those in our Scottish village.

But he was a clever wee chap, who often surprised us with his perspicacity. Bringing him for 10 days to the Isle of Skye, his first real break from home, had seemed perhaps a bit risky. Would he get angsty in this rural environment, with sheep and cows to contend with close to a narrow road? But there wasn't an option really. My mother, who was happily settled in the Victorian house we'd bought a few miles from Stirling, said she couldn't cope with Wallace on her own while we were away. Too energetic.

When I'd first told her we'd get a puppy to make the house seem homier, and to keep her company when we were at work, she imagined we'd buy a lap dog. When we brought Wallace home as an adorable bundle of fluff at just a few months old, everything seemed perfect. But soon enough, Wallace was as far from a lap dog as you could get, always questing after something: restless, inquisitive, a bit like his owners at times! He favoured sleeping on the backs of chairs and sofas, and if something took his attention on TV or out the window, he would do a spectacular balletic leap over the top of whoever was sitting in his way, to get to the floor.

"He'll have my head off one day," my mother would say when he indulged in one of his swan dives.

Jim and I lay awake, listening to rain pattering lightly on the small front window, an owl hooting somewhere and Wallace snuffling about in the bed.

"What do you think he freaked over?" I said.

Jim sighed. "Who knows, but it's an old house. Could be haunted. Perhaps he felt something creepy in the room, especially down near the old empty fireplace. Maybe we should move his bed under the window."

"Maybe."

The cottage was a traditional whitewashed stone construction with thick walls and a corrugated iron roof. It was a solid but modest home and had once been part of a small crofting operation in this part of Skye. We had met the owner, Kathy, briefly when we arrived and she had told us a little about the history of the house, built in 1885. She said that at one point early last century, 13 members of one family had squeezed into the small dwelling, with just two bedrooms and a sitting room/kitchen. Perhaps a few had sadly died here as well. It didn't feel haunted to me, but dogs have different sensibilities.

"We need to ask the owner about the house again if we see her before we go. I'm sure there's a story there," I suggested.

There was no answer. Jim was asleep again and I decided to leave Wallace under the duvet so we could all get some peace and quiet. But moments later he roused himself and, whether he was spooked again or not, he left the bed and skittered and scratched his way down the steps, losing his balance at the bottom, thumping onto the floor and then legging it fast out of the room through the open doorway. He slept the rest of the night on the sofa.

The next day we tried to coax him back into the bedroom, where his bed was still lying near the fireplace. He got halfway in, put his nose in the air, sniffed a moment, then turned and raced back to the sitting room. It was all very peculiar, and for the rest of the stay he wouldn't return. We put his bed in front of the fire, while we decamped to the other bedroom in the attic, up a narrow staircase, where we stayed for the rest of the holiday because Jim wouldn't sleep in the box bed again and Wallace wouldn't sleep anywhere but the sitting room.

Jim and I had visited Skye before, basing ourselves in the more popular central region of the island, dominated by the craggy Cuillins, one of the most spectacular mountain ranges in Britain, along with the famous pointy rock, the Old Man of Storr, south of Portree, which we had once climbed to the base of. But for this trip we wanted to experience the wilder north-west of the island, the Duirinish peninsula, which was over two hours' drive from the arched bridge that crosses from the Kyle of Lochalsh on the mainland to Kyleakin in the south-east of the island.

We'd gone one step beyond wild when we picked a cottage in the west of Duirinish, in Milovaig, a tiny settlement a few miles beyond Glendale, the only real village in the area, with a few shops and cafes and a post office. Milovaig was a scattering of white houses surrounded by acres of grazing fields and moorland, with unforgettable views of cliffs and sea, especially the brooding Dunvegan Head and Loch Pooltiel below. It felt properly remote and cut-off from the rest of the country, which is just what we wanted – for a while.

But there was quirkiness in the scene. On the high cliff-face on the other side of Loch Pooltiel, a waterfall cascaded. When a stiff breeze was whipping in from the Atlantic, however, the waterfall got to halfway down and, as if it had changed its mind on direction, would fan out backwards, up the cliff again.

On the field directly in front of the cottage, black-faced sheep grazed around a stranded fishing boat, a long way from the loch below, seemingly decommissioned forever. On the single-track main road in front of the house was an old red phone box, which was a dead ringer for the box in the 1980s cult film *Local Hero,* set in the village of Pennan, on the northern coastal region of Aberdeenshire. The phone box has become a landmark and was synonymous with the movie.

Because the kind of mobiles we had in the 1990s often had poor reception, we had to use the phone box several times during our stay on Skye. There was something incredibly thrilling about making a mundane call while looking through the glass at a black sky littered with stars, and sometimes shooting stars. It was beautiful and distracting too. It was exactly as the Texan oil executive Mac (Peter Riegert) had experienced in *Local Hero* after he was sent by his oil company to buy out all the villagers so that an oil refinery could be built by the harbour. It was from the phone box that Mac had made regular work calls to Texas and slowly became enamoured of the Scottish village.

This region of Duirinish rivals the north of Aberdeenshire for its authenticity and far-flung romanticism, but like much of rural Scotland, behind the bucolic beauty of the place there is turbulence. For centuries it has been a traditional crofting area, as is much of Skye, where tenant farmers worked their parcels of land and grazed animals, usually at subsistence level. There were around 50 crofts in Milovaig by the 19th century, many of the older ones situated down by the loch and close to the Meanish pier, where boats unloaded provisions and herring was landed. In the past, the croft land was operated on the old 'runrig' system of communal land, where rows were shared out and rotated among 10 or so participating crofters, so that every farmer had a shot at the best pieces of land over the years. It was a successful, fair system, used from the late medieval times.

The older croft houses were built in the style of squat 'blackhouses', like those of the Outer Hebrides, with thatched roofs. Most of these now lie in ruins amid the lower fields after a period of violent political and social upheaval in Scotland. As in other parts of Scotland, the Highland Clearances drastically changed the face of Skye for ever, when crofters were evicted and forced to settle in less fertile areas with less viable plots. The croft houses were burnt, the land cleared for more lucrative sheep farming, and many villagers in Skye, as elsewhere, were forced onto ships bound for North America. This devastation continued here until the Crofters Act of 1886 was passed, which offered a better deal for crofters in rural Scotland, making them freeholders of their land, instead of tenants.

The cottage we were staying in was a former croft house which had survived the worst of the Clearances. Kathy, the current owner and a local artist, had renovated the place some years earlier but kept its original modest style and layout. The attic bedroom had once been for the boys of the previous families, while the girls and adults slept downstairs in the room with the box bed. It would have been a tight fit.

Milovaig was a perfect base to explore this north-west corner, with its famous Neist lighthouse perched on one of the most rugged promontories in Britain. To the south of Milovaig, on wild moorland, lies Waterstein Head, overlooking Loch Mor. There was something about the remoteness of Duirinish, as well as its soft pearly light, that made this part of Scotland seem magical. And the people here, cut off from modern conformity, were often gloriously eccentric and marched to their own beat.

One day on a car trip east we saw a middle-aged woman standing at the side of the road, trying to hitch a ride, which was a curious image in itself. She was dressed in a thick plaid skirt and jacket, with a tartan headscarf and stout boots. We decided to stop and pick her up. I got Wallace onto my lap in the front passenger seat. She climbed in the back.

"Where are you going?" I asked her.

"I'm going wherever you're going," she said, with a kind of rugged nonchalance, which was amusing.

We told her we were on a trip to Dunvegan Castle, a fair drive on the other side of Loch Dunvegan, on the nearby Waternish peninsula.

"Well, I don't want to go to that dreich place. You can drop me up the road at Glendale," she said, which wasn't that far. "I'll manage from there."

Manage?

"But where are you going from there?" I asked.

"Depends who picks me up."

Jim and I looked at each other and smiled. None the wiser.

As we drove along, I sensed a very earthy rural smell about her, as if she lived in fairly tough circumstances, tending a few fields, with a few sheep as well. She had a rough, weathered kind of face but with a great deal of character, and sharp brown eyes. Wallace wasn't sure about this interloper and kept jumping up, putting his paws on my shoulders to get a better look at her.

He growled when she tried to talk to him. He didn't like the sound of her, or the smell either, I imagined.

"Do you always get lifts?" I asked out of curiosity.

"Mostly."

"Aren't there regular buses along this road?"

She gave me a strange look, her eyes like saucers. "A bus? You must be *joking*!" she said mockingly and slapped her knee at the same time with her meaty hand, sending up a small cloud of dust and more rural aromas. Wallace growled again. She told him off, or so I imagined, in what sounded like Gaelic this time, a softer, lilting noise like a command that has no teeth.

"I'm sure I've seen buses pass along the road," said Jim.

"Oh, really?" replied the woman. "Maybe so, but never at the time I want one."

It was hard to say if the service was poor or if she was just being pernickety, or winding us up. It was amusing, if a little perplexing, too.

We had Scottish folk music playing in the car, the popular group Capercaillie, and during a lull of conversation she started humming along with it, becoming more animated as time went on, with plenty of squeals and knee slaps.

"You like this music?"

"Yes, I love it. And why NOT!" she said with a challenge in her voice. She was feisty. "You're not Scottish," she added, noting my accent which, although it's not particularly Australian, isn't Scottish either, apart from the odd word.

"Well, I was born in Perth, on the mainland, so *that* makes me Scottish," I said, with a challenging note of my own now.

She narrowed her eyes at me.

"At least you're not English then," she huffed. "And your husband?"

"Australian," I said, shooting him a glance.

"Good, good," she said. And that was that.

"Struth, an Aussie yet again," said Jim quietly, so she wouldn't hear, flashing me a smile. It was a peculiarity of life in Scotland that while he was working on a Glasgow daily paper, his colleagues would overlook the fact he was English and constantly referred to him as an Aussie, despite him not having much of an accent after 17 years in the country. But in their eyes, it made him more acceptable in an era when there was often some ribbing of English incomers as the independence movement under the Scottish National Party grew in popularity. Though it rarely became rancorous.

She asked our names and I told her, offering Wallace's as well.

"Wallace? Like the Braveheart then?" she scoffed, referring to William Wallace, the Scottish hero.

"Brave sometimes." But not always on this particular trip.

"Mine's Morag MacLeod."

"Not related then to the MacLeod clan of Dunvegan Castle?"

The castle had been the ancestral home of the MacLeods from the 13th century and the descendants were, incredibly, still the current owners. It was said to be the longest inhabited castle in Scotland.

She laughed loudly at the idea she might be related to the castle MacLeods, and slapped her knee again.

"Och, no. Do I look like I'm one of their lot?" she said, thumbing her nose. But somewhere along the line most of the MacLeod clan of Skye would be related, however distantly.

Morag was amusing company and when we got to Glendale I was almost sorry she wasn't going further and that we didn't have time to talk a bit more. I guessed there was an interesting narrative to her life, and stoicism that I could only guess at.

She jumped out of the car, dragging an old leather handbag after her. I caught sight of manly-looking calf muscles below her woollen skirt. She looked like she could round up a herd of African buffalo without breaking a sweat, let alone sheep or cows.

She leaned in to thank us.

"Where do you think you'll go next?" I asked her, pushing the envelope again over destinations.

She shrugged. "Och, how would I know?" she replied, with comical impatience. As long as it wasn't Dunvegan Castle.

We laughed as we drove off. "Do you think she just hitches rides when it suits her, for the company, or could the bus service here be that bad?"

"Bit of both perhaps," said Jim.

When we finally pulled into the car park at Dunvegan Castle I tended to think location was the main thing here, with the castle soaring up from an elevated chunk of rock overlooking Loch Dunvegan. Morag was probably on to something, though, when she described it as dreich (dreary/dismal). Perhaps it was the grey sky above it and a certain mistiness over the loch, but it was a forbidding sight. It was a seeming conglomeration of tall buildings, dating from the 13th century but with a major refit in 1840, which gave the castle a mock-medieval ambience. Perhaps in such an isolated position its flinty exterior was designed to keep intruders away.

We trekked over a stone ramp to the front entrance, described as a colonnaded portico, only to find the castle was temporarily closed. And while we took a breather at the door, admiring the lovely setting and gardens below, I couldn't help but think that with its dreich exterior, Morag would have cut a fine imposing figure at the entrance in her rural plaid, slapping her knee. No devious interloper would have dreamt of crossing the threshold.

Morag wasn't the only phenomenon in this corner of Skye that seemed slightly off-grid. One night, early in our stay, we thought we'd go to a Glendale café that served food and, famously, a vast offering of cakes, we were told. We were the only people in the café when we arrived at 7pm. And indeed, the first thing we saw was the cake collection, which looked out of place in this rural outpost. On several trolleys along one wall there were cakes of different kinds: iced, not iced, fudgy, fancy, and plenty of other fluffy confections, all under plastic covers.

We gawped at this sugary array, for too long probably, and became a bit light-headed and daft with no-one else around.

"Blimey," said Jim. "Look at these! How many cakes, do you think?" I could see his brain whizzing. "So, listen up, here's a little game, if you will, to test your powers of observation and mental arithmetic, okay? If I bought all those cakes and ate half of them, what would that leave me with?"

The answer was simple. "Diabetes, Jim!"

We guffawed for a while, feeling even dafter and probably hungry too – but not for sugar.

A waitress finally appeared with menus but I couldn't concentrate. I was now obsessing over how long the cakes would sit on the trolleys before they became petrified, like jilted Miss Havisham's wedding cake in Dickens' *Great Expectations*. Or if the old oil heater nearby would melt them all first.

I ordered the local mussels with chips, but when the meal arrived, the mussels were grilled, which I'd never had before, and were rubbery, to the point where I had to swallow them nearly whole to get anywhere with them, with the result that I had indigestion half the night. Jim had a steak pie, which was surprisingly tasty, and filling.

"No cake for dessert, Jim?"

"Oh, don't start that."

Though I was dying to ask the waitress who bought all the cakes, I didn't for fear of Jim and me having another funny turn over it.

The cake café wasn't a place we went back to, but I wouldn't have missed the experience for the world.

There were some pretty good restaurants in the general area, featuring local produce, but food isn't what you generally go to remote Skye for, and we were happiest cooking our own simple dinners in the house and eating at the small table by the log fire, with Wallace asleep on the hearth rug. It was a simple but pleasurable holiday, the highlight of which, for me, was walking out the front door every morning to see the same fabulous tableau of the sheep, the backwards waterfall on Dunvegan Head, the stranded boat, the soft pearly light and the often smirring rain, distinctive in Scotland, that falls like gossamer and gives an Impressionistic wash to everything you see.

I was sorry to leave Skye in the end and knew that even though we already lived in a wonderful part of central Scotland, at the foot of a range of low hills with a small castle above a stream, which would give Brigadoon a run for its money, the sheer remoteness and otherness of Skye was truly irresistible, as Harris and Lewis had been, further out in the Atlantic.

Only Wallace seemed relieved to be leaving, having never returned to the box bed room. And when we saw the owner, Kathy, briefly before we left, I couldn't resist telling her about Wallace's skittery behaviour.

"Is the house haunted, do you think?" I asked her, wondering if that wouldn't seem an insulting kind of question. Like "does your house have rats?" or "are the drains defective?" She looked bemused.

"I've never felt it was haunted. No. And no-one else has made that point, strangely enough."

But I pushed on a bit because I knew that some of the descendants of those who'd lived in the house were still in Milovaig. "Do you recall if anything, let's say, unusual or violent ever happened here in past centuries? And forgive my asking."

Kathy shook her head. "I'm afraid I've never heard of anything out of the ordinary, to be honest."

I had expected she might say that, but if something had happened would she really want to tell me? She had a business to run and the house otherwise couldn't be faulted. And not every client would have a journalist's curiosity for the dark side of normal. I let it go, reminding myself that such a lot of violence and upheaval had occurred all over Scotland in past centuries and it's something you still feel in certain places.

Perhaps the paranormal paranoia was ours alone, or perhaps there had never been such a sensitive soul as Wallace staying there before. And it was true of course that most dogs are just wired differently. I had once researched dog psychology for a newspaper feature I was writing under the comical title Do Dogs Need Psychiatrists? One expert told me that a dog's eccentric behaviour is more to do with their physical make-up and the fact that they have such a superior sense of smell that they can detect the remnants of matter that has been dropped and cleared away years earlier, maybe even decades or centuries before. But can they also sense, not so much ghosts, but the remnants, or DNA, of real entities from long ago, those who have lived and died in a particular place?

I didn't share these thoughts with Kathy but I was sure that Wallace's strange behaviour that night was due to something slightly beyond our natural perceptions. Whatever it was, it spooked him completely. We would never know.

Our house near Stirling was of a similar age, with many previous owners, yet we had never felt any kind of strange presence, and neither had Wallace. Or it may have been that all his other eccentric terrier behaviour had overwhelmed anything of a spooky nature. There were people who found Wallace himself quite spooky, not to mention stroppy, including a grumpy emergency plumber who brandished a spanner too quickly, the outcome of which was Wallace nipping his bum, which fortunately didn't lead to an injury or legal action. However, I have to confess that as well as Wallace feeling uncomfortable with the man, oddly, so did I, even before the spanner was raised.

On the drive back home at the end of our stay on Skye, as we reached Glendale village, I noticed Morag standing outside the post office near the road, talking to another woman. Morag had her big leather bag at her feet and was standing with her hands planted on her hips, her legs slightly apart, which made her look stockier and solid, like a Sherman tank in plaid. We stopped to beep the horn and say goodbye. She grabbed her bag and rushed over to the passenger side window. I told her we were leaving.

"Do you need a lift somewhere on our route perhaps? We're going back to Stirling," I said.

Her eyes danced with interest. I almost imagined she'd say "Stirling, please". I hoped she might want to go some of the way, so I could have a last blether with her on the long drive home. But she shook her head.

"I'm getting a bus home," she said brightly.

What? A bus? "I thought you said there were hardly any buses along here?"

"Och, there's never a bus till the moment you don't think you care about a bus, then there'll be a bus. There's a bus on the way, see," she said, pointing east to a speck way in the distance that looked nothing like a bus.

My head felt giddy with her logic, the way you do in rural Ireland when you ask someone directions that lead you into a tiring maze of left-field thinking.

"Okay, Morag. We're off then. It was lovely to meet you and I enjoyed our brief talk the other day. Take care."

I held my hand out the window and she grasped it, giving me a rugged handshake. I could feel tough, calloused fingers, leathery palms. "You too, lassie, and Aussie Jim," she said with a wink in his direction. "Come back one day. I can gi' ye a few more stories."

I looked back at her in the wing mirror as we drove away. She was standing by the road, watching our car head off, or perhaps she was still staring towards the speck of bus in the distance. At one point she waved, as if she knew I was watching her. But how could she?

What I didn't know then was that some years later, in the wild Mani region of southern Greece, where Jim and I would live for a time, I would, in the most peculiar case of doppelgangerism, meet Morag's Greek counterpart. She was another incomparable, feisty rural woman, called Foteini, a goat farmer and literary muse of sorts, who would feature in the Greek memoirs I would write.

She was made of the same stoical stuff, with the same big meaty hands, but with a palpable softness to her and quirky view of life. As with Morag, I would meet her on a village road, but Foteini would be on a donkey. And with a nod to her alter ego, Foteini had a curious predilection for wearing thick tartan shirts. It would be a strange thread running through my life, connecting disparate journeys that would seem more coincidence than design. But then how can you ever know?

Chapter 6
Castles, craic and cantering
(Galway, Ireland)

IN A pub in County Galway an old man called Finlay, with a head of thick white hair and wearing a warm tweed jacket, was sitting at the table beside us. He was full of the craic, engaging us in all sorts of conversation, some of which we struggled with due to his heavy but tantalising accent. He was drinking Guinness, as were we.

He nodded his approval at our two frothy glasses.

"I'm glad to see you're drinking the Guinness," he said with a wink. And before we could respond he added: "Ah, the Guinness! You see now, it's the best thing for ya. It's the best thing for when you're feeling happy. Sure, it makes you more happy. And it's the best thing for when you're feeling low. Now it's a great thing if you've got a cold. It takes it right away, and it's a great thing if you're getting over a cold. Magic. And to be sure, it's great to drink if you even *think* you could have a cold coming on, you see. Magic again."

He was smiling and sipping away, like the best kind of advertisement you've ever heard for Guinness, the health remedy. Who knew? I imagined that even if you just visualised a glass of Guinness in your mind, according to Finlay's theory, it would fix everything from ingrown toenails to insomnia. Magic!

I've always loved an Irish yarn and Irish logic for the fact it's often charmingly askew, but all part of the banter here. Basically, the Irish like a good blether and tell a good story. And with the accent, well you could listen to them reading a long shopping list and it would sound like Yeats. And garrulous characters like Finlay were easy to come by in any pub in Ireland.

Jim and I were on a week's media trip from Scotland, organised by the Glasgow paper Jim was working on. We were staying at Ross Castle, 12 miles north-west of Galway City, run by an ebullient American couple, millionaire George McLaughlin and his ex-concert pianist wife Elizabeth, both originally from New Jersey. The castle, built in the 16th century, was an important historic pile and the story of why this couple bought it in the mid-1980s was as interesting as the site itself, which we would later hear more about.

Jim and I could have flown from Glasgow to Knock airport, in nearby County Mayo, but we decided to add a few more days to the trip and take our car on the ferry from Stranraer, in the west of Scotland, to Belfast, and see some of Northern Ireland on the way, driving through County Down and Armagh and the northern swathe of Ireland.

While Northern Ireland had been comparatively peaceful since the Good Friday Agreement in 1998, there were still sporadic incidents taking place. Six years after the Agreement, as we were heading through the verdant countryside of County Armagh, there were chilling reminders of the Troubles. A huge grey slab of a building stood by a main road, and it was a police station, massively fortified with barbed wire and cameras, like something from a World War Two prisoner-of-war camp. Further down the road, we had to slow down dramatically when we came across a group of heavily armed British soldiers patrolling by the roadside, searching the undergrowth. It was a small and perhaps insignificant manoeuvre but gave a tiny insight into how difficult daily life must have been here in the past. While the countryside was nevertheless appealing, we felt more relaxed after crossing the border into southern Ireland on our way to Galway.

Ross Castle, with its 120 acres of land and clipped, emerald-coloured lawn undulating down to a private lake, seemed like another world. The building was a five-storey pile, with a slew of stone outbuildings, once stables and servants' quarters, now renovated and let as separate cottages and apartments, one of which we were staying in for a week .

On the second day of our stay, we were invited to the library in the castle to have a proper chat with the McLaughlins over coffee and club sandwiches the size of breeze blocks. The couple were generous and wonderfully garrulous, especially Elizabeth, who told the story of how they came across the castle and the fact that their first intention had been to buy a holiday house, so they could spend more time in Ireland and reconnect with their Irish roots. It set me wondering how big a holiday house they first had in mind.

"We looked at a few different properties and weren't intending to buy a castle at all, but when we found this one, with its own lake and the whole place ringed by these lovely hills, we were very keen. But it was in a ruined state. It hadn't been touched since the Great Potato Famine of 1845. It had no roof, floors or windows. It was just walls with views," she said, expansively, throwing her arms wide and laughing. "But what views!"

George nodded dreamily while munching on his sandwich and was maybe reflecting on what had driven him, a top-flight boss at IBM in Manhattan, to spend his millions on a shattered pile in Ireland, when he could have stayed in comfortable New Jersey. The couple's strong Irish roots, as well as their connections with the Irish communities of Boston and Philadelphia, obviously informed the castle-buying narrative, and I got the impression that Elizabeth had been in the driving seat. George admitted he'd been happy to defer to her on matters of interior decoration, as she'd had something of a flare for it in America.

Predictably, the project turned out to be much bigger and more expensive than anticipated and cost 3.5 million euros over 15 years, due to the amount of structural work to be done on the buildings. The castle had been built in 1539 by one of the more colourful dynasties of Galway, the 'Ferocious O'Flahertys', and in 1590 it was bought by the Martin family. In 1770 much of the interior and roof was destroyed by fire, although the roof was replaced. The castle had been left empty and neglected for many decades, until the McLaughlins hoved into view. It is now an exquisite showplace, with much of it operating as a holiday-let business.

"It's a monster to run, as you can imagine," said George. "The cost of the oil heating is about 30,000 euros a year at the moment and will probably go up over the years."

I asked Elizabeth what had happened to her music career in the meantime.

"Oh," she said, becoming more subdued. "Well, I had to give it up professionally when we came here." And if there were regrets about that, she wasn't saying. But one rainy day, when we were mollaching around our apartment in one of the renovated outbuildings, we found a hoard of newspaper clippings at the top of a wardrobe and brought them down for an inspection. There were stories about some of Elizabeth's first recitals in the 1960s and 70s, when she played at the Carnegie Hall. Photos showed an elegant, accomplished woman seated at a grand piano at the start of what could have been a distinguished career. Easy to see it might not have been comfortable talking about what she gave up, though few people wouldn't envy their life now in the renovated castle, with its vaulted ceilings, exposed beams and a collection of fine furniture, mostly brought from their home in New Jersey.

But there was only so much castle we could gaze at and we were keen to see some of the area's beauty spots, such as the wild cliffs of Moher on the west coast of County Clare. The cliffs, 700ft high in certain places, are 320 million years old. But perhaps the most spectacular sight for me on that visit wasn't just the cliffs and the wild Atlantic sparkling on a sunny day but a completely eccentric Irish family lying on a deep, flat, grassy ledge accessible by a path from the clifftop.

Two adults and four children were lying on the grass in a semi-circle, holding hands and staring up at the sky, blethering and laughing madly, with a sheer drop to the rocks below, just a few feet away from the toes of their walking boots. It looked like some kind of west coast ritual, or rite of passage. It was one of the funniest sights I've seen, and peculiar even on Irish standards.

The other place we wanted to visit was Connemara, in the west of County Galway, where we'd already booked an adventurous horseback trail ride. This region is small but packed with character, a mountain range called the 12 Bens, rust-coloured bogs, sheltered coves and horses, of course. But Connemara is more than just landscape: it's a centre for Irish music and language, has buzzy pubs serving local seafood and was the location for much of the filming in John Wayne's famous romantic comedy *The Quiet Man* in 1951, with Maureen O'Hara.

Much of it was filmed in villages not far from Ross Castle, and it apparently still attracts John Wayne fans, who end up trail riding to beach locations, trying to capture the west coast/cowboy essence of the movie. There really is something about Connemara that makes you want to get out in the thick of it on the back of a horse, which is why we'd booked a two-hour trek from a riding centre in the fishing village of Cleggan, where chaps and cowboy hats were optional. We settled for the regulation hard hats.

Jim and I had learnt to ride in Australia before we left in 1999, but while Jim hadn't kept up the lessons in Scotland, I had gone every week for a couple of years to a slew of local riding schools and had become a proficient rider after having to negotiate everything from stroppy ponies to bucking ginger mares. Then there were the massive Clydesdales, far too big for my short stature and a bit like riding a padded camper van with big feet.

Jim was feeling excited but also nervous about the trek, as he hadn't ridden in months. He was given a 17-hand gelding called Seamus, while I had a smaller gelding, about 15 hands, called Rory. Ned, the instructor, wasn't what we'd expected – but is anything in Ireland? While he tacked up the horses he told us he was a lobster fisherman most of the time and a riding instructor part-time. He was easy-going and dressed not in any kind of riding gear, or fishing garb either, but a scuffed leather jacket, jeans and loafers, and his position on the saddle was so laid-back he sometimes looked like he was reclining on a sunbed. The fact Ned wasn't wearing a riding hat either seemed in keeping with his nonchalant vibe.

We took a riding track from Cleggan over the fields towards the coast, where we would join a causeway at low tide and ride to the small tidal island of Omey. Nearer the coast we switched to narrow roads, though we rarely saw a car. The spring weather was gorgeous and warm. Now and then we had a canter along the road. The rhythmic drumming sound of hooves on bitumen, and the sight of the Atlantic sparkling in the distance, was one of the sensations of this trip I'd never forget. Ned was, despite everything, a good rider, as if he'd been born on a saddle. The only hiccup on the way was that Jim's horse, the more solid looking, was angsty at times.

"Don't hold the reins so tight," Ned told Jim, stopping us for a minute. "That's what you've probably been taught, isn't it, to keep a tight rein? But Jayzus, we're on a country road in western Ireland, the horse knows his stuff, right, he won't bolt wit' ya, okay now?"

Jim nodded, then shot me a tentative look. We continued the ride for another 10 minutes, but Seamus was still jumpy, tap dancing a bit when there was a strange rustling in the bushes because horses, despite passing bushes every day of their lives, can act as if they've never seen greenery before, or birds, rabbits and so forth. And they're basically wind-up merchants, too.

"Seamus is sensing we're getting close to the sea," explained Ned, "and he's anticipating a nice gallop over the sand towards the island is what he's doing. But don't let him push you about, okay. You're in charge."

Jim mouthed "As if!", in my direction when Ned turned his horse towards the beach.

"Don't worry. It'll all be fine," I said confidently, even though I'd never had a flat-out beach gallop before, and neither had Jim. But this was Ireland, home to horse whisperers and champion riders. It had to be done.

When we arrived at the beach, Ned had a plan, however. We were to change horses, and I imagined he was going to take Seamus, because he knew all his wily ways. But instead I was to have the big angsty beast and Jim was to ride Rory, whom I'd become rather fond of. So we changed horses, and Jim looked good on Rory, and more confident.

"I hope I'm not too big for him," said Jim to Ned as he settled himself into the saddle.

Ned gave the pair of them a cursory glance. "Maybe a bit, but look on the bright side, you won't have so far to fall from him. Though you won't fall, of course, will ya?" he said, with a roguish grin. I guessed this was one of his regular wind-ups with less experienced riders.

Jim and I exchanged jittery looks and then we laughed. What else could you do? I had the opposite problem, however. I felt tiny on Seamus, like an afterthought. And I could feel him jittering under me, keen for his beach gallop, and that was probably all his bad behaviour had been about, the excitement of it all. But I'd be lying if I said that galloping on Seamus didn't seem edgy. Together we'd look like a Riverdance performer, a blur of jittery movement from the waist down, frozen on top.

The sandy causeway was wide at low tide and it was a good distance to the island, which lay low in the water, a flat grassy mound. We trotted for a bit, so we could get the feel of the horses, with Ned out in front. The moment he picked up the pace on his black gelding, the other horses followed. We had a slow canter and then the horses gunned themselves into a gallop. It felt fast, scary and unstoppable, charging over the causeway, kicking up sand, between stranded seaweed and half-buried boulders that I watched out for in the beginning, wary of a stumble. After a short while there were too many and I gave up looking for obstacles. That was the point where I started to really enjoy the wild freedom of a beach gallop. To hell with everything else!

As a learner, there's a point where you just have to trust the horse and go with it, even if it means forgetting some of the finer points of riding along the way.

When we were close to the island, Ned turned his head slightly towards us, as if to check we were still there. He looked anxious and brought his horse slowly back to a canter, then a trot, and circled round towards us. We also slowed down and finally stopped, slightly out of breath, smiling broadly.

"That was fantastic, Ned," Jim said, his cheeks flushed with excitement, pleased he'd handled his first real gallop.

But Ned ignored him and looked at me.

"Jayzus! I turned there a minute ago to check you both out and Marjory, *you* were up in the saddle like you were riding a winner at the Grand National. You don't need your backside that far out of the saddle. Jayzus, we're only doing a beach gallop. It's a good way to go pingin' off. I'm thinking I need a wing-mirror on my horse to keep an eye on you," he said, rubbing his horse's neck as if planning where he could put it.

The image of his horse decked out like a Harley-Davidson made me laugh rather too loudly. Nervous laughter!

"I'm sure my bum wasn't that far out of the saddle."

"It feckin was, trust me!"

Jim shot me a look and I could tell he was holding back a guffaw, no doubt glad it wasn't him being reprimanded.

"But Seamus," I said to the horse, "you didn't let me get pinged off now, did you?" I ruffled his mane and he side-ogled me with interest, snorting loudly.

Ned smiled. "Okay, I see he's happy with yourself. No harm done. Just keep your arse down on the way back, okay?"

We cantered the rest of the way to the end of the strand, where the horses took a well-worn track onto the island. It was bigger than it looked, with an expanse of machair, the grasslands prevalent on the west coast of Scotland and Ireland, and wildflowers were in abundance. A path wound around the island past a central lake and a view towards the mainland of the 12 Bens of Connemara.

There are ancient remnants on the island of 7th century villages and the church of Saint Feichin, thought to mean 'little raven' in Gaelic, for reasons that are now lost to us. The church, possibly part of a larger monastery, attracted monks over the centuries, drawn to the remoteness of the island. The church lay for centuries buried in a sand dune but was partially unearthed in 1981, though mostly just the stone walls.

Even today the area is about as wild and windswept as you will find in Ireland, with nothing but the sight of the sea ahead and the sound of an Atlantic breeze hissing lightly through the machair. I could feel Seamus instantly relax beneath me, nickering softly, unafraid of bushes and birds, as we plodded along the pathways. It seemed like the most enjoyable way to tour a slice of untouched Ireland. Perhaps it was for this island refuge in particular the horse had been champing at the bit to get to.

We also rode past a graveyard, thought to be around 1,000 years old and used by island residents. In the 19th century there were around 400 people living here but the potato famine of 1845 forced most of them to emigrate. When we were on the island, there was just one, a part-time resident called Pascal Whelan, who'd spent much of his time in America as a film stunt man. He was rarely seen here and when he died in 2017 became the last person ever to be buried on the island.

On the way back to the mainland we had another gallop across the beach, on which I managed to lower my bum on the saddle and got a valiant thumbs-up from Ned, without the benefit of a wing mirror. The trek was more relaxed on the return, picking up the same pathways again, with Ned out in front and Jim and I riding side by side, chatting. We were rosy-cheeked and euphoric from our riding adventure.

Learning to ride in adulthood had been no small achievement for either of us and every manoeuvre accomplished, every scary ride survived, would always bring endless satisfaction.

On a forest trek once, as a novice, with a Scottish riding instructor, I'd jumped for the first time and fell off the horse onto hard stony ground. Though I was badly bruised, but with no bones broken, I thought the incident would set me back a bit so early in my riding endeavours, and yet it didn't.

"You have to work through the pain barrier to acquire riding skills," the instructor had later said, and not just on a physical level. She believed that riding was a metaphor for dealing with all kinds of risk taking. "Modern life is so predictable you need to take risks to discover more about yourself as much as anything, as you do on the back of a horse." The whisky-filled hip flask she carried around on treks probably helped with the pain barrier too and on one occasion at least I had need of a nip myself.

Back at the riding school, Ned seemed to be in a rush. He suggested we might like to untack the horses and give them a rub down if we had time.

"It was grand to meet you both today, but I have to run now. I've got a few lobster pots to sort out for the fishing tomorrow." And off he went. It seemed like a fitting, and slightly mad, ending to an outstanding afternoon.

The next day at the castle we were saddle sore, and after breakfast we asked Elizabeth if we could try out the indoor swimming pool, in a separate block at the back of the castle, to loosen up a bit.

"Not at all. As long as you don't mind sharing it with Father O'Reilly," she said. "You see, Father O'Reilly is our local priest and he always comes once a week off-season for a constitutional dip."

Sure enough, as we were doing a few laps in the pool, with its glass enclosure giving lavish views towards the hills, Father O'Reilly stepped shyly into the pool area, dressed in a black cassock, holding a rolled-up towel.

"You don't mind me joining you now, do you?" he asked in a soft burr.

"No, of course not," we said, slightly amused at the idea of swimming with a priest. Dressed in his cassock?

I was mulling this over when he walked to a chair in the corner of the pool area and, with his back to us, started to slowly take off his robe. I averted my gaze, and twitched my eyebrows in Jim's direction, but he was watching Father O'Reilly as well, wondering no doubt, as I was, whether he had his swimmers on underneath or not. After a few minutes, the priest turned and made his way down the steps into the pool, wearing baggy knee-length swimmers, his torso and legs as white and smooth as a pint of milk.

He gingerly began to do a slow breaststroke on the opposite side of the pool, his head above the water

Jim had a certain glimmer in his green eyes and I knew he was feeling mischievous.

"Will you be blessing the water for us, Father?" asked Jim boldly, with a surreptitious wink in my direction.

"If that's what you'd be wanting, then I'll be doing that as I'm swimming along," replied Father O'Reilly, with a serene smile.

"Do you like to swim, Father?" I asked him, imagining most Irish priests probably wouldn't be inclined.

"Oh, I do, yes. It's like this, you see. While I'm swimming along I feel I'm clearing my mind of all troubling thoughts, feeling closer to God, especially when I can swim in *complete* silence." His eyes flickered towards me.

Oops! Jim grimaced in my direction. Were we being reprimanded for chattering? My heart sank. Then Father O'Reilly guffawed.

"Okay, I'm just saying that to tease yourselves. I don't mind a bit of craic in the pool, as long as I'm not going to be asked for confession. No, I don't do confession in the water." We all laughed.

He was good company but after a while we decided to leave him to his quiet contemplation and return to our apartment. We waited until we were inside to have a good chuckle.

Ireland, what a treat: priests blessing swimming pools, lobster fishermen on horseback, concert pianists living in castles, funny old guys promoting the dubious health benefits of Guinness. It's a place where you never know who or what the sunrise will bring you. And, to be sure, it won't be what you're expecting.

Chapter 7

Lairds and local heroes
(Morayshire, Scotland)

WHEN I was commissioned by a Scottish newspaper to interview Ninian Brodie, the clan chief of one of the oldest families in Scotland, at his 12th century pile in Morayshire, I jumped at the chance.

On the long drive up through spectacular Aberdeenshire to Brodie Castle, set amid 175 acres, I tried to conjure up an image of what the laird at 87 would be like. Without the benefit of internet archives in the late 1990s, I only had access to some out-of-date news clippings, and the little I'd read depicted him as a genial but slightly eccentric aristocrat, whose life in later years had been rocked by a family scandal. To help with my research, I'd spoken to a few prominent people in Aberdeenshire who'd met him. His profile wasn't as predictable as I'd expected. He was posh of course, educated at Eton, and a great character, but I was thrown when I heard he'd studied acting and had a wicked sense of humour. So, no ordinary Scottish toff then.

He would have needed the sense of humour because he'd had to sell the castle and its contents to the National Trust For Scotland (NTS) in 1978, which in the following decades ignited bitter family rows that inspired headlines in the national newspapers. None of his family and descendants would ever call the castle home, apart from Ninian Brodie himself, the 25th Brodie of Brodie (as the lairds here are called) who, as part of the NTS deal, was allowed to live out the rest of his life in one wing of the property. He'd also agreed to act as a consultant and guide for visitors, a task he took on with great relish.

During the years I worked as a freelance journalist in Scotland from 1999, I'd had a crack at some quintessentially Scottish stories, all of which I'd loved. In a bid to re-establish some links with my homeland, I couldn't have picked a better way to go about it. The stories had touched on the political evolution of the country at the time, with the start of devolution.

I also interviewed a vast assortment of people, from politicians to equestrians, healers, adventurers and Scottish authors, but Ninian Brodie would stay in my imagination for quite a long time, one of the most unique characters I'd ever met. And the castle itself, in rugged and remote Morayshire, east of Inverness and below the Moray coast, would also leave a lasting impression.

I met up with a local freelance photographer in the Brodie Castle car park. Angus had been here before and was laid-back about the castle façade, but I was instantly taken with it. Although in theory it's classed as a 'tower house', it was hugely impressive with its slightly pink-tinged, lime-harled walls, pointy towers and ornate battlements.

We were welcomed into the grand entrance hall by one of the staff, a middle-aged woman in a smart suit. I had expected she'd escort us to one of the castle's many public rooms for the interview, but she took us to a small table near the entrance, where an old gentleman in a kilt and tweed jacket was sitting, and introduced him as Brodie of Brodie, the current laird. The woman then disappeared, along with a few American visitors, whom Brodie had been regaling with a few anecdotes.

There was an easy charm about this octogenarian, with his dark hair and moustache, and bright inquisitive eyes. And he had plenty of energy, bouncing out of his chair to greet us with a vibrant smile. I thought of the description given to me by a local journalist while I was researching Brodie: "He may have gone to Eton and mixed in rarefied circles, but he's no snob. He's really quite a normal fellow."

Perhaps not terribly 'normal' but he was certainly hugely likeable. He apologised for wearing a red and blue hunting tartan kilt and tweed jacket and not his smart Brodie dress tartan. He was colourfully attired, however, with a red and white striped shirt, red tie and green socks.

Then he treated us to an amusing tale about why the dress tartan kilt had been abandoned. "It was handed down to me by a shorter relative and now it no longer fits. At my age I don't want to be seen in a mini-kilt," he said, laughing uproariously.

He kicked off a short castle tour by walking us first around the vast entrance hall, with flagstone floor, wood panelling and Romanesque Revival columns and an impressive marble statue of the Medici Venus.

There was also a formal portrait of Ninian Brodie. While we stood beside it, he said: "I often sit at the desk by the entrance and people come in and look at this portrait here and then look at me and don't realise I'm

Brodie of Brodie. When they do, they're always amazed. I say to them, 'Yes, that's me in the portrait, and that's one of my ancestors over there'." He pointed to the opposite wall.

We swivelled round, expecting to see another august painting of a fine figure in a kilt, but instead he was indicating a bronze sculpture of an orangutang.

Brodie's face creased with laughter. "That's one of my little jokes."

Angus, the photographer, began to snap away, grateful for all these comical flourishes, which showed that at a great age Ninian Brodie hadn't forgotten his earlier dalliance with the theatre. Although he'd had to give up acting in his 40s for his ancestral obligations, the castle was at least a big enough stage for him to strut his stuff, and his castle tours were said to be quite theatrical, with the benefit of the odd risqué limerick. I asked Brodie what was the importance of the orangutang in this grand space.

"Ah, you see, George the orangutang was always an obliging character and the sculpture was used as an extra 'person' at the dining table whenever there was an odd number of guests. It was thought an odd number was bad luck. So there you have it," he laughed, enjoying himself immensely.

He took us to some of the most impressive rooms in the castle: the Red Drawing Room, the Blue Sitting Room, exquisitely furnished, and a formal sitting room containing some of the castle's vast collection of paintings, including Dutch masters and artworks by the Scottish Colourists. There was a large painting of King Charles I by Van Dyck, given by King Charles II to Alexander, the 15th Brodie of Brodie.

Indeed, it's when you see the artworks and other treasures around the castle you realise how intricately this family was involved with Royalty, and other major figures from British history, from the family's beginnings in the 12th century. The Brodies, for their loyalty, were given the land by King Malcolm IV in 1160 and the earliest laird recorded is another Malcolm, the Thane of Brodie, whose position in Morayshire was validated by King Robert the Bruce, hero of the Battle of Bannockburn, in the early 14th century. The family's successive allegiances gave them much prestige, but also considerable grief, with huge setbacks and debts. In the 16th century, Alexander Brodie had his lands forfeited by the Crown through his involvement with a rebellion against Mary Queen of Scots, though the land was returned to him four years later.

While a fortified tower of some kind had been on this site since the 12th century, most of the current building was started in 1560, with stunning square towers, turrets and battlements, and finished some seven years later. The extensive alterations to the house and gardens over the centuries led to crippling debts, especially a makeover in the 18th century by William, the 22nd Brodie of Brodie. It was only William's marriage to an heiress that prevented the whole estate from being sold.

The library is by far the most impressive room, with some 6,000 books in fine wooden bookcases. It was here that Brodie showed us one of the castle's rarest items, a framed letter written in Latin by King Robert the Bruce, which Brodie was especially proud of. In the sepia tinted but legible note, the King is writing to Malcolm the Thane of Brodie about the maintenance of the castle, and he instructs him to take better care of the mill pond, as its neglect has annoyed the neighbours, the monks at Pluscarden Abbey, near Elgin. Built in 1230 as a Benedictine monastery, it survives to this day and is the only medieval monastery in Britain still used for its original purpose.

While I sensed Brodie's obvious delight in owning this letter, one of the few from Robert the Bruce still in existence, the rest of the vast history encapsulated in this castle seemed to sit light as a feather on his tweedy shoulders, though a final segment of the tour later on would reveal a slight crack in his armour.

We moved on to the northern wing of the castle, his wing, for the interview. The sitting room was a homely abode, with a fireplace and chintzy sofas and chairs, the walls covered in old paintings and prints. He offered us some red wine, apparently a mid-morning ritual, though the photographer and I had to drink judicially as we were driving.

With a glass under his belt, Brodie relaxed even more, if that were possible, as he was one of the most laid-back lairds you could imagine. He was good company, happy to reveal as much about his colourful life as we wished to hear – and more besides.

The photographer and I were sitting on the broad sofa opposite Brodie, who became more animated as he sipped his wine. At one point he got up and sat on the arm of his chair, with a series of old documents and maps of the castle spread over the floor in front of him, about which he'd been explaining some historic details. He suddenly started to lose his balance, tipping backwards, legs slightly splayed, and we were faced with the sight of crisp white underpants, though of course we quickly looked away to spare his dignity.

Angus winked at me as Brodie quickly righted himself on the arm of the chair, none the wiser, laughing off his wobble. And so one of the greatest questions foreigners ask about the Scots was answered: Do they really wear nothing under their kilts? The answer is 'no'. Not for this particular laird, anyway.

The habit of going naked below, or 'going commando', relates back to the dress codes of the highland regiments, some of whom demanded that nothing be worn beneath, for reasons no-one seems to grasp now. When the Scots first wore kilts they were more practical plaid items, made with a longer length of heavy material, one end hanging over the shoulder, the other gathered at the front and fastened with a belt. The only 'underwear' of former centuries was a long shirt worn underneath the kilt. The kilt was often used as a kind of blanket when highlanders had to sleep out on the hills.

The more we got to know Brodie, the more I felt that had he gone commando it wouldn't have seemed at all peculiar, as he was a rather unconventional soul, which I sensed he must have inherited from his mother, Violet Hope. She apparently had a passion for toads, naming two of them Volumina and Cleopatra, and also reptiles. But while Violet had a healthy sense of fun and eccentricity, she didn't approve of Brodie's desire to become an actor after he left Eton. His father Ian had tried to push him towards some business enterprise, but when that failed to find favour with young Brodie, he was allowed to pursue acting.

"My father just said to me, 'Well, do it then because you have to do something'."

Brodie had an early life typical of the Scottish aristocracy. While he was born in the castle and lived there until he was nine, he was then sent to boarding school in England and only returned on summer holidays. He remembered those early castle years fondly, with vast grounds to roam, and the lovely atmosphere of the castle, lit by candles and paraffin lamps. In the 1930s he studied acting in London and later performed at the Old Vic and in repertory companies, including Perth in Scotland, where he met his wife, actress Helena Budgen, whom he married in 1939 in London, with Hollywood star Stewart Granger as his best man.

It was also in Perth that was told of the death of his elder brother Angus in a car accident in 1937. In a cruel twist of the saying 'be careful what you wish for', Brodie explained: "When I was younger, I used to be so jealous of Angus because I always assumed he would be the next Brodie of Brodie when my father died. Angus's death was the great tragedy of my life."

A dark shadow seemed to flit over his lean face with the memory of it and what came later. Brodie had been stationed in North Africa in World War Two when he heard of his father Ian's death, and 10 years after the war he returned home to take control of the castle with his wife Helena.

However, by 1978 it became clear that the crippling maintenance costs of the castle were too much and he decided to sell it and its priceless contents of furniture, paintings and archival treasures to the NTS for £130,000.

His woes might have ended there, had it not been for the fact that some 18 years later younger family members were now unhappy about the former sale of the property, in particular his son Alastair's children: Alexander, Phaedra and Edward. In an astonishing move, the grand-children sought legal advice to investigate the sale and the fact that the price, they believed, was lower than the property was worth. They took their grievances to the Edinburgh Court of Session (the supreme civil court) to have the sale annulled.

"I am fighting for my rightful inheritance," Alexander was famously quoted in press stories in the 1990s, though the grandchildren eventually lost the case. The situation sensationally reared up again in early 1999, when Alexander, then living temporarily in the castle, had to be forcibly evicted, and in protest spent several days sleeping rough in the castle graveyard, which grabbed headlines in Scotland and in the national papers.

A Guardian story called it "a tale of fallen aristocracy" and Alexander at least must have garnered some sympathy with his struggle to hang on to his birthright.

When I broached the subject of the grandchildren's revolt over the castle, Brodie, for the only time that day, said he wasn't happy to talk about it much.

"It's all been said now, I think. It's been in all the papers from Buckie to Brighton, I believe, and it's a bit raw for us here. But what I will say is that the farcical thing is they (the grandchildren) are fighting for something that no longer exists. They are fighting over valuables and the castle, but all that could be theirs is an empty castle and no money to run it. I wasn't sad handing it over to the NTS. It has now been restored, and it was a great relief really. We didn't realise how bad the roof was and the south turret was hanging on by a thread."

When I finished the interview, he invited us to stay for lunch in the small dining room on the ground floor, where he usually took his meals.

"I expect you've still got a few more questions," he said, sipping the last of his red wine.

The lunch invitation was unexpected and not a usual part of this kind of interview session. As we made our way down to the dining room, with Brodie strolling on ahead, Angus whispered to me in his broad Aberdonian accent: "You know, in all the years I've worked on newspapers up here, I've never been asked to lunch, not in a castle anyway. This is a first."

But to me it felt that Brodie was that kind of guy, a laird with a big, convivial heart.

On the way to lunch he detoured to the formal dining room in the castle, which we hadn't yet seen. It was wood panelled with an intricate carved ceiling, shutters and great style. It also had quite a few portraits by prestigious artists of the many generations of Brodie lairds. They were hung around the walls and one in particular, from a few centuries back, looked incredibly like the current Ninian Brodie.

I commented on that and he stood a moment, contemplating the portrait with a rather introspective look. "Yes, you could be right," was all he said and I detected a hint of something I would have described as regret. I wanted to pick up on it, but thought it would keep for now.

Lunch was a jovial affair, two courses including roast lamb and more wine. Brodie talked in animated fashion and reminded me that I'd heard stories that during his castle tours he often broke into amusing thespian flourishes to bring the castle's history to life. And the history was immense, as the Brodie lairds were involved in historic and religious events in Scotland down the ages. In the 18th century the family rallied against the Jacobites, who supported Bonnie Prince Charlie in his bid to re-establish the reign of the Stuarts. The 19th Brodie Alexander was a great supporter of the government troops led by the ruthless Duke of Cumberland, who defeated the Scots at Culloden. It has been documented that Cumberland's troops had been allowed to rest in the castle grounds on their way back to England after the battle.

There have also been myths and legends associated with Brodie Castle and its surroundings. A hillock a few miles away is known as Macbeth's hillock and is believed to be the "blasted heath" of Shakespeare's *Macbeth*, where the three witches foretold Macbeth he would become king. Shakespeare based the play loosely on the real Macbeth, king of the Scots in the 11th century, who was born in Morayshire.

After we finished dessert, with a delicious slice of apple pie and cream, my thoughts were tugged back to the formal dining room and the portraits of Ninian Brodie's ancestors. I wondered what it was like to be Ninian, to live in a castle where all your forebears had lived since the 16th century, with connections to the land going back even further. Not many people, outside the Royal Family, can claim that. Or to see the cast of characters involved lined up in one room of the castle. I wanted to broach the subject that had been nagging at me from earlier.

"What's it really like being part of such a long, colourful dynasty as this?" I asked, with the kind of awe reserved only for ordinary outsiders like myself.

Angus shot me a look, as if I'd strayed onto a difficult path, and yet it seemed perfectly valid to me. As a local snapper, however, Angus obviously knew more than I did about all the struggles and frailties of this Scottish aristocrat. Brodie became suddenly quiet, and the shard of that regret I'd seen earlier darkened his eyes. He fiddled with the spoon in his empty bowl.

"It's an honour being part of this great family and its history, of course. But as for my actual place in it? I don't think I've achieved very much. I haven't done anything. I've managed the castle these past few decades and I'm proud of that, but I didn't start any of this," he said, with a gentle shrug.

I could well imagine the subtext to this comment was that Ninian Brodie, after handing the castle over to the NTS, would always think of himself now as the Brodie who, sadly, lost the castle, and who had to sell it. It was the elephant in the room. But we had to leave it there.

Eager to change the atmosphere, he said: "Now, I'll tell you something that might amuse you. Remember the dinner service we saw on the table in the dining room? It was a fine import from China by Alexander Brodie in the 18th century. The service has our coat of arms on it and our motto, Unite, but several pieces of the service were misspelt with the word 'Untie'." He laughed heartily, appreciating the irony, the Freudian slip perhaps of a 102-piece dinner service surviving with a nod towards the fate that would engulf the castle and its inhabitants with historic missteps, debts, family revolts, and finally that sale to the NTS. But it was of no matter now.

When we finally made our way back to the entrance hall, Angus and I were in no hurry to leave. We had stepped outside our normal lives for a brief moment and experienced something we would never experience again probably: a rare glimpse into the rarefied world of Scottish aristocracy.

"I expect you have a last question?" Brodie asked, with a twitch of amusement in his eyes, because he was no stranger to the wiles of journalists.

"Well, one flippant question perhaps. Does the castle have a ghost?"

He smiled. "No, I don't think it has, but there's a secret passage in the castle. I didn't show it to you because it's so secret none of us can ever find it! That's another of my little jokes. I always tell visitors that one and it gets a laugh." And right on cue, we did.

On a more sentimental note, he added: "When visitors express disappointment at our having no ghost, I say that's because it has always been a happy house."

Perhaps there was some truth in that, if you can forget all the historic turmoil and personal battles that have swirled around it at times, like a North Sea mist.

As we left finally, mid-afternoon, Brodie stood at the main entrance, waving goodbye. He was a slight figure, dwarfed by the size of the turreted pile behind him, and I thought that although he'd had to sell his birthright, and maybe a piece of his soul along with it, he'd hung on to his sense of humour at least, and his optimism.

I had planned to drive to Aberdeen that night to break my journey back home, but as I was feeling weary after a big lunch, I decided to stop in nearby Elgin for the night.

Elgin is one of the loveliest towns in this part of Scotland, famous for its distilleries, cathedral and Gordonstoun School, where the then Prince Charles was sent and hated its Spartan qualities, and also where prominent, contemporary British novelist William Boyd boarded for a time, and also had mixed feelings about the place.

I stopped for the night at a B&B near the town centre. In the early evening, still full after lunch, I accepted a sandwich and a mug of tea for dinner from the owner of the establishment, Isobel McIntosh. I was pleased to learn there was no potato soup bubbling on the back burner in her kitchen, as I'd experienced at a hotel in Durness when I took my mother on our highland jaunt a few years earlier.

Isobel asked me why I'd come to Elgin on my own. I told her about my interview with Ninian Brodie. She was impressed

"So, what did you think of him?"

"I liked him a lot. He's a proper gentleman, but there's no airs and graces about him."

"Well, there shouldn't be, eh? He handed the lot over to the National Trust, didn't he?" she said, hands on hips. "And what a stoushie with the grandchildren and all that, trying to snatch back their inheritance. Most unsavoury."

"You could say he did a good turn really and the castle and its historic contents are now secure for the nation."

She harumphed a bit. "Yes, I suppose that's a lot better than it being sold to some rich pop singer or such, contents and all!"

And that was my last thought of Brodie Castle, imagining the sound of a loud, ramped-up guitar riff sweeping through its salubrious corridors, shaking the priceless heirlooms, and rattling the dinner service with the motto Untie.

* * * * *

The next day, waking up refreshed after a deep sleep, I fancied taking a detour on my way home, as there was much in this area I wanted to see. Now that I was here, I decided to drive to the coast, north of Aberdeen, to visit Pennan, the famous fishing village that was one of the locations for the iconic 1983 film *Local Hero*, directed by Bill Forsyth. I wanted to see if the village in the flesh had any of the quirky atmosphere of the film nearly 20 years on.

The route to Pennan is a long, winding drive through a quiet rural landscape which brings you finally to a cliff top, with the vast expanse of the North Sea ahead. A steep road leads down to the village. The minute I was out of my car I felt a strange detachment from the rest of the country. This traditional fishing village is a simple, long row of whitewashed houses set under a rugged grassy cliff. Like many villages on the north coast of Scotland, the houses are built close together and set with their gable ends facing the sea, to avoid the worst of North Sea weather. They dominate the scene, along with the tiny harbour at the eastern end, where much of the action in the movie took place. Nothing much here seemed to have changed.

I had planned to talk to some of the residents and perhaps write a freelance piece on the village, but I imagined the residents here might be tight-lipped or jaded talking about the film now, even though it had put the place on the map. But as I casually wandered about, I found people raring to blether about the subject.

One woman called Elspeth, originally from Aberdeen, who had moved here with her family and was now working as an artist, told me candidly: "We're all nutty here. It's very alternative. A little bit of the world where you can be yourself."

Several others I spoke to seemed to back up her claim. No surprise really, as *Local Hero* was quirky, with comical characters like Gordon, the publican who opens the pub when he feels like it and doubles as the village accountant. There's a touch of magic realism with the attractive mermaid who regularly pops up at the harbour, the love interest of one character at least.

And of course there's the eccentric American oil types who want to buy the village, called Ferness in the movie, to turn it into a commercial venture. The fishermen depicted in the film (many of whom were village extras) are endearingly aimless, hanging about the harbour at all hours in their rugged Aran knits, blethering on about nothing in particular, and look like they wouldn't know one end of a trawler from the other. The whole vibe of the film is amiably crackers.

There's no doubt *Local Hero* changed the place from a traditional community, where resident fishermen battled with the perishing North Sea to make a living and wouldn't have had the luxury of being quirky. But the film aura has dug itself in over the years, while fishing has decreased, and has lured incomers from other parts of Scotland and England, who make a living renting out rooms in Pennan or being arty, like Elspeth. Many have bought houses as holiday homes and come for a few weeks a year. There were only 15 full-time residents, I was told at the time of my visit, a small fraction of what the village would have originally supported. Some people admitted there was friction now and then between locals and incomers, understandably perhaps, but not enough apparently to dent its appeal. And after the film crews left in the 1980s, the residents said they all felt like movie stars for years afterwards.

Elspeth said that a few years after the film came out she was in a taxi in London during a visit to the capital. "When I told the driver I was from Pennan, he asked me for my autograph. I was mortified, but that's the sort of reaction you got."

The reality of living in Pennan in the late 1990s was less glamorous perhaps, with few facilities. When I visited there was no shop, and only one pub, although it's a star turn on its own, with a Scottish Film Council plaque on the whitewashed wall outside flagging up *Local Hero*.

The publican of the Pennan Inn, Norrie, was very proud of its role in the film and tried to keep the spirit of it alive, with a slew of framed photos in the bar of its stars: Burt Lancaster, Peter Riegert, Peter Capaldi, Denis Lawson. And there was other memorabilia, such as the production notes from the film, which Norrie kept in a box behind the bar. Across the narrow road was the iconic red phone box, which is now, incredibly, an official 'listed building'. The phone box was where Texas oil company executive Mac (Riegert) made his frequent calls back home.

Mac was lured by the simplicity of the village, the people, the ceilidhs, the Northern Lights, and he quickly soured over the commercial reason he'd been sent: to buy up the place to build an oil refinery. The Pennan Inn has always been the centre of this village, as it was in the film, and still is in the present day. Norrie said that after the film was released the village attracted hordes of visitors. And in the ensuing decades it was still the same.

"Wherever the film is shown in the world," said Norrie, "whether it's Japan or Australia, people start arriving soon after. They have this ritual here. Visitors stop their cars at the top of the brae, turn up the Mark Knopfler soundtrack (from the film) really loud and drive into the village. It's madness. It's almost like a religious experience." (Even today, though Norrie no longer runs the pub, I recently learnt film fans still keep coming, though in slightly fewer numbers).

Norrie was originally from Edinburgh but took over the Pennan Inn when it came up for sale, to have a complete change of lifestyle – and that's what he got. It was very communal and, yes, quirky.

"Often we'd have guests upstairs in one of the pub rooms and we'd run out of food for breakfast, so I'd go and raid neighbours' fridges for food. People never bothered to lock their doors, so I'd just let myself in. That's how we lived."

Norrie agreed that despite the *Local Hero* association, the village was a place where anything was likely to happen, the madder the better.

He told me a story about four trawler fishermen, young guys, in the days when less punishing fish quotas meant fishermen in this part of Scotland could make outrageous sums of money, though it was hard work.

"So, these four fishermen turn up in a flashy black car and come into the pub. They leave the car outside, with the engine still running and all the doors wide open. Not sure why, maybe they weren't planning to stay long. The group orders pints of lager with large whisky chasers, and after a while they're a bit blootered (drunk) and debate whether to head home or not. The driver goes out and kills the engine and comes back in for another session. He apologises for their behaviour to a handful of other customers watching all these antics, saying, 'We've just been two weeks at sea and got a massive catch of monkfish, so we're feeling good and having a wee drink'."

Even on this short visit, there was undeniably something special about Pennan, a bit of Scotland cast adrift but sprinkled with celebrity stardust, a case perhaps of reality imitating fiction over and over. Mac, the film's hero, once he discovered Ferness, didn't want to go home to Texas at the end. Many of the residents expressed the same sentiment and apparently would tell visitors not to leave, as they did with me. "Stay and have a drink, stay for a week and then you'll know what Pennan's about," said one, as if once you've arrived there, time takes on a different meaning. I didn't doubt it.

Yet I did leave, facing a long drive that day, though I was tempted to stay the night out of sheer practicality. As I drove out of Pennan in the afternoon, my car groaning up the steep brae, a sharp North Sea wind was whipping up waves, sending a cloud of fine sea spray across the narrow strip between sea and houses, and it felt colder. I expected to meet another car at the top, with its engine gunned and a Knopfler track turned up to the max, but I saw nothing but green fields beyond.

The quirkiness and the glamour of Pennan would perhaps live on several decades more, then likely burn off in the end, like a famous Aberdeen haar (fog). But one thing wouldn't fade, and that was the absolute splendour of this corner of Aberdeenshire, which I hoped would survive intact, with its film fantasy, its wind-blasted glamour and its legends, much like Brodie Castle will for another few centuries.

* * * * *

A few days after my story about Ninian Brodie had appeared in a Scottish daily paper, he sent me a card. It featured one of the family portraits from the castle, typically not of himself, but of Hugh Brodie the 23rd laird as a child (in the early 19th century) with his brother George, both dressed in kilts with a highland landscape behind them. Inside, he'd written a note thanking me for the article, which he'd very much enjoyed. Brodie also candidly told me he'd gone out the day of publication and bought 12 copies of the paper to 'impress' some of his friends and family. The card was a kind gesture and typical of him.

Ninian Brodie, the inimitable 25th Brodie of Brodie, and the last of his family to ever live in the castle, sadly passed away in March 2003. When I heard about Brodie's death I realised how lucky I had been to spend even that short time in the company of this unique and genial character, the like of which will probably never grace a Scottish castle again.

Chapter 8

There's heaven in Hellas

(Paxos, Greece)

W E WERE cruising our small motor boat into the village of Lakka, with its pretty harbour lined with neat white houses, cafés and tavernas. The place was buzzing with early summer holidaymakers, and along the quay a row of boats were moored.

"Let's tie up there and jump ashore for a Greek coffee, as you do. How about it?" said Jim, piloting the boat.

"Can you do that? Isn't it beyond novice boating? I mean, I'm thinking of all the things Babis told us, and I don't remember mooring the boat in a busy harbour being one of them," I replied.

We'd never rented a boat before. In the UK, you'd have to jump through a few hoops to hire a boat if you had no experience. In Greece, all things are possible, and health and safety, in 2006 at least, wasn't festered over, not on a tiny island like Paxos.

Paxos island is just south of Corfu, in the Ionian islands. As it's only accessible by boat it has given a swerve to mass tourism and is still fairly traditional and remote, a fact that has lured celebrities over the years, such as Angelina Jolie and Keanu Reeves. More recently, however, in 2023, its beauty and charm catapulted the island to sudden fame with the hit Greek series on Netflix called *Maestro In Blue*. Filmed on Paxos, it features Greek actors in a surprisingly explosive storyline - for a quiet refuge like Paxos at any rate.

In Paxos, we hired a boat with a 30 horsepower engine, called the Glaros, Seagull, from a boat-hire guy in Loggos harbour, a tiny fishing village further south, where we were staying. Babis gave us a half-hour of instruction on mechanical and boatie things and where to go and what to do.

"Don't go on the west side of the island, beyond Lakka. It gets too rough, okay?" he warned.

He told us to anchor the boat properly if we were stopping in bays for a swim or a break, and to tie the boat up as well.

"Never leave it drifting, not even in calm weather."

In Greece, he explained, the weather could change in a heartbeat from calm to windy to wild. And I'd seen it often enough, especially on the islands.

We set off from picturesque Loggos, with its small quay and gentle curve of harbour, its tavernas and white houses backed by olive groves. We turned north past deserted, pebbled coves with clear turquoise water and thick swathes of olive trees in the hinterland – olive oil production being one of the island's main industries. We planned to stop in one or two coves on our way back later, for a swim, but for now we were keen to explore the east coast.

We were heading for the bigger harbour of Lakka, in the north, where we thought it might be cool to moor the boat and stop for a coffee at a waterside café and lug into the boatie crowd. But when we cruised into the deep, horseshoe-shaped bay, with the harbour at its head, it looked even bigger than we'd expected, and busier.

I glanced at Jim, as he quietly steered. He was looking ahead towards the crowded quay, scraping his teeth over his lower lip.

"Do you know about mooring, Jim?" I asked lightly, not wanting to make him feel nervous, or to skewer the illusion that boating is a 'man thing', and therefore always under control. It especially applied to this location, which in mythological terms was the haunt of the macho sea god, Poseidon, and became his love refuge as well.

When Poseidon had once seen the enticing sea nymph Amphritrite dancing with her sisters at a mainland location, he was so smitten he requested her company, but she hid from him. When she was eventually found, she was brought to Poseidon in nearby Corfu by a kindly dolphin.

But Poseidon, in a bid to keep her a secret from his wife, slammed his famous trident, the three-pronged spear, down on the southern tip of Corfu, breaking it off and creating Paxos, with its smaller nearby sister Antipaxos, though in the process he sadly dropped the trident, his weapon of choice, into the sea.

As I mused over Greek sea gods and mythical trysting, we were drawing ever closer to the quayside, where only one narrow space seemed available, next to a large, flashy motor cruiser.

With his eyes on the space, Jim steered the boat slowly towards it. The mooring looked tight, but if it was also dodgy, Jim was saying nothing about it. The cruiser was on our starboard side, and even before we got to it, we heard a load of hollering coming from above, at the stern of the vessel.

"Cut the friggin' engine and get your bloody boat away from my water line, you total twat!" an Englishman yelled in a Home Counties accent.

We both looked up and saw a rotund, menacing guy in a baseball cap, leaning red-faced over the rail of the cruiser.

"Is he shouting at us, Jim?" I asked, slipping up to the tiny wheelhouse.

"Bugger! I've come in a bit fast and close to him," Jim said, frowning as he sized up the plastic line draped down the side of the cruiser, then arcing under the water and up, at an awkward angle, towards the pier to some kind of water tank for refilling. But what did we know? Not much. As we drifted further in, the guy started up again.

"Move off now! Your propeller blades will cut my friggin' line, you moron!"

Jim cut the engine and we drifted slowly towards the quay.

"Okay man, chill! Engine's cut!" shouted Jim, waving dismissively towards boatie beast, who scuttled along the side of his cruiser like an angry crab, his eyes glaring down at his precious water line for any hint of damage.

Jim seemed calm and in control, but when we neared the quayside he turned to me and rolled his eyes. "That was close, Margarita."

Jim calls me Margarita in Greece because that's what Greeks always call me. It's easier for them to say than Marjory because despite speaking the second hardest language in the world (Japanese being the first at that particular time), Greeks can struggle with a few letters in English, like the 'j' sound, which always makes me smile.

I've always loved the name Margarita, apart from the fact Jim often gives me the moniker when he's trying to make a serious point, or when he's annoyed, or flustered. He was obviously rattled over the mooring.

"Now, Margarita, you'll have to jump the gap onto the quay and I'll throw the rope. You can pull the boat in a little. It will be easy, okay. I need to stick by the controls."

I went up to the bow and stared across the gap.

"Are you kidding me? I can't jump that far. It's at least three feet. I'm short and petite, remember?" Long jump had never been my specialty at school, but nor had high jump either. I had no intention of ending up in the water. "You'll have to do it, I'm afraid," I offered, slinking back from the bow.

Jim got up with a heavy sigh. That's when I noticed that just about everyone lolling about the outdoor cafés on the quay had lugged into the mooring drama and were probably waiting for us to do something diverting, like crashing the boat into the quay, or me plunging into the harbour. There were smiles all round and a couple of ill-concealed sniggers.

"Okay, okay." Jim went to the bow and looked about. "Just don't touch any of the controls."

"As if!"

He pursed his lips just before he did a balletic leap onto the quay and gently pulled the boat closer. The café crowd were simmering down but the guy on the motor cruiser was still fuming, and still checking his water line with his dark wingnut eyes.

As I clambered onto the quay, Jim was busy tying up, twisting the rope around a bollard with a certain flair.

"I didn't know you could do fancy nautical stuff like that."

"I can't. I haven't got a clue, but this looks okay."

I smirked as we sat down at a nearby café, with small tables under sun umbrellas. I noticed, as we ordered two plates of galaktoboureko, the rich custardy sweet renowned in Greece, and two coffees, that Jim never took his eye off the rope, in case it somehow slithered undone and the Seagull drifted out into the harbour – or into the side of the cruiser.

A man at the next table must have noted Jim's obsession with the bollard.

"Proper job in the end," he said, with a strong Cornish accent, smiling impishly. "But you haven't been on boats a lot, I take it?"

"Oh, less than an hour, that's all," said Jim, consulting his watch.

The Cornish guy, who looked and sounded slightly seafaring, mustn't have had a clue about the brevity of Greek boating instructions. He choked a bit on his fizzy drink. I laughed. That's what I love about Greece, a place where adventure comes to you, never the other way round. And the day was so young!

Refreshed from our Lakka stop, we were nevertheless relieved to be pulling out of Lakka harbour a while later. We decided to be sensible and not go round the top of the island, to the western side, where the Ionian Sea, as Babis hinted, might be too challenging. We cruised down the coast again, looking for a quiet cove for swimming. We found it some 20 minutes later, a wide cove with a pebbly beach. It was wonderfully tranquil, backed by bushes and tiers of olive trees. We dropped anchor close to the beach.

"Babis said we should always tie the boat up as well," I reminded Jim, having annoyingly recalled Babis's short list of dos and don'ts.

"I don't think we need to tie the boat up here. We can jump in for a swim and sit on the beach for a bit. The weather's really calm."

"Whatever!" I said, taking off my shorts and T-shirt, ready to jump in. The water was so blue and inviting, clear enough to see fish streaming by.

Jim got ready for his swim. Then he stood with hands on hips, deep in thought.

"Actually, I suppose we should tie it up. It would just be our luck for some rogue wind to blow in and pull the boat about on its anchor, or worse." He sighed.

I jumped off the boat first into cool, clear water and splashed about. Jim followed, holding the mooring rope. We headed for the beach first and looked around for a place to tie up the boat, like a tree trunk. There wasn't much. As we were sizing up possibilities, one of the bushes at the back of the beach began to rustle. We both jumped as a naked man walked out and came towards us. He was pale, with longish hair, sporting a big, pendulous penis, a frightening site in this remote location.

"Nudist beach," said Jim with a grimace. "Good choice, eh, Margarita?" I nodded, hoping that's all it really was.

The man walked over to us with an inquisitive look on his face, but all I could see was his awkward, half-deflated tumescence.

I felt I should tell him off for exposing himself but some gremlin in my head had other ideas. "So, after all those centuries, it seems you've found Poseidon's missing trident, and it's a bit worse for wear! I see there's two prongs missing!" I scoffed.

The man put his hands on his hips and looked flummoxed. Not a follower of mythology then. Jim gave me a dark, keep-quiet-now look.

Nudist man ignored me and turned to Jim. "Are you looking for somewhere to tie up your boat," he said, his penis swaying awkwardly in front of us, like a drunken gatecrasher at a wedding reception.

The man had said his piece though without any hint of irony. Dead serious. Jim and I looked at each other, forcing down a fit of giggles.

Suddenly another figure broke free from the bushes: a naked woman, broad of beam, with droopy breasts and what looked like a Brazilian shave below. Jim coughed nervously. Easy to see what had been occurring in the undergrowth.

"What's happening, Jeremy?" she mewled.

"These people need a place to tie up their boat."

"Not any more we don't," Jim snapped, turning quickly towards the water, holding the rope and tugging me along by the elbow.

"I just wanted to help," girned Jeremy loudly behind us.

"Save it!" shouted Jim, guiding me into the water. "Let's push off. This cove's a nuthouse."

We dived into the water and as we neared the boat, we burst into loud hysterical giggling, while the nudists stood side by side on the beach, watching us, mystified perhaps that we wouldn't take up the man's dodgy mooring offer.

We scrambled into the boat and pulled up the anchor, raring to go.

"What did they have in mind, Jim?"

"Don't even ask, Margarita. And Babis has a lot to answer for, with all his ridiculous rules, tying up and so forth. And there was me thinking the Greeks don't like rules."

Further down the coast we found another cove, seemingly deserted. We dropped anchor and swam ashore, with no thought of tying up this time. We inspected the bushes, just in case, and found them clear of nudists. After a long, refreshing swim, we sat in the shade of an olive tree to eat a few peaches we'd bought in Lakka and drink some bottled water.

"That was close, with the nude guy, eh?" Jim said.

"Yep," I replied. "Never seen a stranger mooring bollard in my life."

Jim chuckled. "You know what? I didn't think that hiring a boat was going to be this odd, and troublesome."

By mid-afternoon we'd arrived at the capital of Gaios, an appealing harbourside town full of neat, white- and gelato-coloured houses, with quiet streets and charming shops and restaurants. In those days it attracted Greeks from the mainland and other visitors but in fewer numbers, including a small contingent of boatie types. We had moored easily this time at the quieter edge of the harbour, opposite the small leafy island of St Nicholas, and walked a few minutes into the town.

We had lunch at a traditional taverna, with its mix of locals and tourists. The tables were set under a large blue canopy. We ate Greek salad and fried fish, with a small bottle of beer each. As the afternoon ticked on, diners slowly disappeared for a siesta, but one table near the front door was lively, with half a dozen old Greek guys drinking ouzo, talking and laughing, and two were playing the board game, tavli. They were making quite a noise, but we liked it. It felt real.

When the noise of the old guys reached a certain crescendo, however, the owner of the place, a woman wearing a white apron and a scarf around her hair, burst onto the front veranda, her hands firmly on her hips, and spoke to them in Greek. Having learnt some Greek in my younger days, when I lived for a year in Athens, I had kept it up with various classes in different places, and I could get by with easy conversations.

"Don't go shouting and laughing like crazy people in the summer. It's fine for us, but you'll frighten the foreigners away. See, they've all gone already," the owner implored them, her eyes sweeping the near-empty terrace. "It's all right in the winter, when there's no tourists about. Now go home and have a siesta, or keep quiet."

I was amused and surprised that Greeks would be told off, on small authentic islands like this, for enjoying themselves in summer. But it's something I later came across in other parts of Greece, where men in the winter were allowed to enjoy their bibulous nights in tavernas and the old-style *kafeneia*, which years ago were men-only hangouts, but in summer they had to disappear to secret back-street haunts.

The old guys looked across at us. One hunched his shoulders in our direction, arms out in a 'what can we do?' gesture. One touched his lips theatrically with his finger. We laughed and shrugged back, showing their antics weren't a bother to us.

Paxos is a beautiful island, with the tiny sister islet of Antipaxos nearby. It has a remote, authentic feel, with small harbours, numerous idyllic coves and traditional villages inland with old-style tavernas. The island has the easy rustic feel of places I remember from youthful Greek holidays. The island still has only 2,300 permanent residents, and is just six miles long by two miles wide. It takes only a few hours to walk the length of it, mostly through tracks in the vast olive groves.

We had rented a village house on a hillside not far from Loggos. As the harbour area had so few parking spaces, we had to walk down the *kalderimi*, cobbled donkey track, to reach it, shining a torch on the trek back to the house after dinner, which added a hint of romance and atmosphere to the whole proceedings.

The house was called Thekla's Cottage, after an old-fashioned female name, which suited the house perfectly. It was a solid stone dwelling, about 100 years old, whitewashed, with green shutters and a large terrace with sea views. The place hadn't been modernised much. The furniture was dark and heavy and most surfaces were covered in embroideries of indeterminate origin, and folky wall hangings were also a feature.

The kitchen was small and functional but felt like it had been plucked from another century, as was the water situation. Due to a lack of a natural water supply on the island, rainwater was captured in roof gutters and fed into underground tanks in most houses. This meant it could become slightly brackish and couldn't be safely drunk after storage. During periods of drought, water had to be delivered to the island by trucks.

While everything was comfortable enough, and not lacking in authentic atmosphere, the real problem was the beds. The main double bed had a rock-hard mattress probably decades old and was sunken in the middle, like the bed in the movie *Psycho*, where the mad mother was supposed to sleep. Jim claimed it was crippling his back, and my neck was aching so much after two nights that I had to wear one of those blow-up neck supports you use on planes to aid sleeping.

We abandoned the bed and migrated to the spare bedroom, with twin beds, until we decided the Psycho bed was the 'best', if that were even possible. It was not since our stay at the old Scottish croft house in Skye, with its challenging box bed, that having a sound night's sleep had become such a thorny issue.

But the redeeming feature of this property was the large terrace, with views to the sea, shaded by olive, orange and kumquat trees, full of the little orange citrus fruits that originated in China before they were introduced to the western world. The fruit is much favoured by the Corfiots, who use it to make the island's famous kumquat liqueur. On the first night that we ate on the terrace, we were startled by pinpricks of light in the darkness all around us.

"Jeez, I feel like I've got detached retinas looking at those lights. What are they?" said Jim theatrically. We followed the lights around the garden until we realised they were fireflies. Despite the many times I'd visited, and worked in Greece too, I'd never seen fireflies before. They were mesmerising.

Another night we were visited by a large and ancient-looking hedgehog, which came barrelling down a long pathway and stopped at the table, and bristled, as only a hedgehog can. We had moved the table slightly and we were blocking his usual evening run, it seemed. There was always something skittering in the undergrowth as well.

One evening at sunset, after having had a quiet, romantic dinner on the balcony, I saw something shimmying in the trees.

"What are those things in the kumquat trees, swinging on the branches?" I asked Jim, pointing to the edge of the terrace.

"Don't know. Some kind of small furry thing, like a squirrel or marsupial?"

I racked my brains for a small animal with a long thin tail.

"They're not furry critters. Bloody hell! They're rats!"

We walked to the trees to investigate in the dimming light and could see their dark solid shapes and their beady eyes, as they swarmed amid the branches, grabbing at fruit.

We grimaced to each other.

"That's horrible," Jim said. "I hope they're not planning a full-scale rodent incursion into the house."

The next morning, we met up with the cleaning woman, Katerina, a local Greek, who came to the house three times a week to tidy up and sweep and wash the terrace. She also took away our bags of rubbish because finding, or using, rubbish bins in Greece is often a dispiriting business, as well as the frequent lack of collection.

Katerina was a genial soul, who liked a chat, her arms crossed over the top of her broomstick, and she was happy to let me practise my rusty Greek.

We asked her about the rats.

"Pah! Don't worry about them, they're *xenoi* rats, they won't bother you."

Xenoi is the Greek word for foreigners, strangers, outsiders. It made no sense for rats. I asked her what she meant. "Are they foreign rats here on holiday?"

She laughed heartily. "No, what I mean is they come out from the orchards and the hills, they come now to feed on the kumquat fruits and later they will go back."

So, interloper rats, I think she meant. I tried to explain it to Jim.

"Margarita, aren't all rats interlopers? I mean, no-one ever *invites* them, do they?"

I sniggered. "No, of course they don't."

"Ask Katerina if they will come into the house if we leave windows open during the night."

She screwed up her face at the question. "No, they won't, but don't ever leave your windows open."

"Well, that means 'yes' then, doesn't it?" said Jim, rolling his eyes.

I had a feeling we would lie awake most nights while we rolled into the bed's Psycho dip, imagining rats scraping around in the kitchen or eating ancestral furnishings, of which there were quite a few.

The next morning Katerina came by unexpectedly with a neighbour, who wanted to meet us. He spoke reasonable

English but with a heavy accent. We sat on the terrace for coffee and some honey cake, which he'd brought with him. Yiannis was a tall, well-built man, retired now, but he'd had various jobs in the past: in the merchant navy, olive farmer, café owner, builder.

We talked about Paxos, his ancestral home.

"It's a beautiful island. Not developed like Corfu, but we are going in that direction now," he said, waving his arm towards a few houses along the narrow road through this rural outpost called Dendriatica (Place of Trees). Here, foreigners had seen the attraction of this small island and had started buying old village wrecks to renovate and sell as holiday homes.

"We are covering our island now with *semen*," he said, with emphasis.

I looked at Katerina. She only had a scrap of English. Jim raised an eyebrow at me.

Seamen, I was thinking, because the island had become a retirement mecca for sailors, perhaps, like he'd once been.

"Sorry, we don't know what you mean, Yianni," I said.

Jim decided to pitch in. "Ah, you mean the people living in these renovated houses … are indulging in, em … too much, em …"

I cut Jim off quickly. "No, Jim, he doesn't mean that."

Yiannis sighed with impatience. "It's easy word. You know, building the houses with all the semen."

"Ah, got it. You mean *cement*," said Jim, looking more flustered than he had at mooring a boat.

"Yes, that is what I said, of course. These people are covering the island with semen, building and rebuilding houses. Too much for a small place. It will all spoil."

Jim and I smiled at each other over this language gaffe, of which I had committed many in Greek over the years.

But in terms of Paxos, we felt it was a long way off being spoilt, not compared to other islands, and the vast swathes of olive orchards would save it no doubt.

It was partly our chat with Yiannis that inspired us before we left to check out some of the refurbished houses that were up for rent, particularly long-term. Having had several Greek holidays while we'd lived in Scotland, to Corfu, Santorini and Kefalonia, we toyed with the idea of one day, a few years in the future, taking a year out to live and freelance in Greece. It's a country we were both very fond of, but me especially, having spent a year in Athens after leaving high school in Australia, and having had many long trips back to Greece .

While we loved our life in Scotland, I feared we were both growing restless again and keen for another adventure, even short-term, while we were still young enough.

One circumstance in particular had made me feel less settled. A few years after we'd arrived in Scotland, my mother Mary, with whom I was very close, had sadly passed away. It was a devastating loss for me after bringing her with us back to Scotland, a move she had fully embraced, despite some initial misgivings.

My mother's death had also loosened my ties a little with the country. While we stayed on in our Victorian home, we had no reason to stay there permanently, and a downturn in the newspaper industry in Britain had hastened our desire to move, for a while at least. Paxos was certainly a contender for a mid-life adventure. The island was remote, still very Greek, and it seemed perfect. However, as things turned out we chose a very different location in the end.

Before Yiannis left that day, we asked him about the water, since we knew he also served as a bit of a handyman around the place. We were keen to know why the water in the bathroom shower was turning our silver jewellery black. We showed him the rings and silver medallions we were wearing.

He shook his head, suggesting there must be something wrong with the water heater in the bathroom. "It is very old and needs to be replaced."

"Is it safe?" I asked him.

He pulled a face. "Yes, but don't wear the jewellery in the shower. I will bring you something to clean the jewellery. Are you down in Loggos this evening?"

We told him we'd be at one of the tavernas opposite the harbour, sitting outside.

"Okay, I find you."

While we were having a meal that night we saw Yiannis passing by in his van. Unable to park at the harbour, he stopped nearby and waved us over.

"I have something for your jewellery." He handed us a package, which was a handful or two of white powder wrapped in cling film. He told us it was bicarbonate of soda and how to use it on the silver.

A group of English visitors were strolling past and gave us a very odd look as we examined the package of white powder and nodded at Yiannis's instructions. I offered him some money but he batted it away.

As Yiannis roared off in his van, Jim quickly pocketed the powder.

"Jeez, I hope no-one thinks we were doing a drug deal with Yiannis. That's what it must have looked like, eh? Cocaine in cling film."

"How do you know about that?" I asked him, with a teasing look.

"Oh, don't be daft now. I've seen it in movies." We laughed on the way back to our table in the taverna, wondering why it hadn't looked odd to Yiannis the way it did to us. But Paxos was hardly the drug capital of Greece.

We had a laugh about it over dinner, and later on we tried out the silver 'polish', not that it made a lot of difference. For the rest of our holiday I was terrified of what the water might contain and if our hair would fall out before we left.

"What if our teeth go black? What might be lurking in the water tank?"

Jim shook his head. "I hate to think."

On our last night in Paxos, at our favourite taverna at the harbour, we got into conversation with a couple at the next table, English tourists, also staying in Loggos. The man, called Jerry, asked us what we'd done on the island and we mentioned our boating adventure.

He told us they too, as total novices, had hired a boat out of Loggos from Babis. They had gone one step beyond us, however, with their motor boat and bravely decided to go further south, to the smaller island of Antipaxos, famed for its outstanding white sand and starling turquoise water. It was slightly foolhardy, the man admitted.

"We had been warned that the crossing could be choppy by mid-afternoon as various sea breezes start to blow in. But the morning we went the water was pretty calm and it only took around 20 minutes. That wasn't our biggest problem though. When we got to Voutoumi beach, there were several boats anchored in the cove and quite a few sunbathers on the beach.

"I wanted to get close enough to anchor, maybe tie up the boat somewhere, like Babis advised you as well. Trouble was that I forgot, in my panic over the crowded beach, to drop the anchor and I misjudged the speed I was doing and how far away to cut the engine. Long story short, I ended up ramming the boat up the beach, with people jumping up and running away. It was chaos for a bit, like a kind of Normandy Landing."

We all laughed at that, especially Jim, who was probably thinking that his mooring effort in Lakka was a snip compared to this guy's wartime manoeuvre.

"We survived all that," Jerry explained, "but then the return journey wasn't great either. The water did get choppy, with a load of spray over the bow. We were late getting back. When we arrived at Loggos, Babis was stalking up and down the pier, waiting for us. He was a bit angry, as we were well past our agreed time.

"Babis said, 'You know, my friend, for a while I thought perhaps you had done something crazy like take the boat down to Antipaxos, but I told you not to do that, not as a novice'. He gave me a shrewd look and I think he knew that's exactly where we'd been. I just shook my head and said, 'Oh, Babis, I'd never do anything like that. A man has to know his limitations'. Ho, hum!"

We all burst into gales of laughter at that one. To this day, when I think of Paxos, I recall the boating mishaps – ours and Jerry's. It still makes me smile because deep down we all love those who occasionally flout their limitations and do something impetuous or crazy, and live to tell the tale. After all, it was a subject I knew more than a little about, and not just on Greek shores.

Epilogue

IN 2010, after 11 years in Scotland, Jim and I rented out our house and left for a mid-life adventure in Greece, with our irrepressible terrier Wallace. We didn't go to Paxos, however, we went to a completely different location, to the wild Mani region of the mainland's southern Peloponnese.

After a harsh winter, a British recession and a downturn in the newspaper industry, it seemed like the perfect time for a Greek odyssey. The fact that Greece had just slipped into an economic crisis of its own failed to dent our enthusiasm, as we planned to write feature articles for various publications, often charting the effects of the crisis.

One year quickly became four as we enjoyed the lifestyle, as well as the company of the many Greeks we met, even during this difficult time. We did, however, return to Scotland and sold our property, moving to England, to Cornwall in the rugged south-west, where we currently live.

After several serious moves in my life (and one or two others there hasn't been scope to mention in this collection), I feel certain the shoogly circle of migration and uprootedness that preoccupied me in earlier years may now be closer to completion. Whether or not we stay where we are or undertake another move is yet to be seen.

But one thing is clear: despite my wanderings, Scotland remains a special place for which I have the strongest sense of belonging, despite not living there at present. The road north to Scotland will always be an irresistible lure, and it takes but a moment to fire up the electric bagpipes on the car's sound system!

The Peloponnese series

If you enjoyed this collection of stories, you may also enjoy Marjory McGinn's four Amazon best-selling travel memoirs, set in Greece, for which this book is partly a prequel.

The Peloponnese Series – *Things Can Only Get Feta, Homer's Where The Heart Is, A Scorpion In The Lemon Tree* and *A Donkey On The Catwalk* – charts Marjory's four-year adventure, living in authentic villages in southern Greece during the economic crisis. The books are written with the author's typical good humour and memorable insights into a rural Greek way of life that is slowly disappearing, and includes a cast of heart-warming Greek characters.

The books are available from all Amazon stores (Kindle ebook and paperback) and selected independent bookstores, and Barnes and Noble.

Praise for Marjory McGinn's
Greek travel memoirs

"**Gerald Durrell meets Bill Bryson.**" Goodreads reviewer.

"**Marjory tells a good story with a journalist's eye for mood and detail.**" Alex Martin, Anglo Hellenic review.

"**Entertaining, informative, enthralling.**" Peter Kerr, *Sunday Times* best-selling author.

"**I loved the characters and the enthusiasm that drives the narrative. What an adventure!**" Mark Douglas-Home, best-selling author.

"**This book (Things Can Only Get Feta) might become a future reference source about life in unspoilt Greece.**" Stella Pierides, poet.

"**Wonderful books. When I read them I am walking and living the journeys.**" Amazon reviewer.

"**I could read this series forever. The author's books have brought humour, knowledge and good people.**" Patti Wilson, Amazon reviewer.

"**I have read a lot of travel books and Marjory McGinn is one of the best writers in this genre. She keeps your interest all the way through.**" Amazon reviewer.

"**The author is an excellent ambassador for Greece.**" Valerie Poore, author.

The Bronte in Greece series

Marjory has also written two Amazon best-selling novels set in southern Greece.

A Saint For The Summer takes place in the wild Mani region and is a contemporary tale, combining family drama with a gripping narrative thread going back to World War Two. During the Battle of Kalamata, described as the 'Greek Dunkirk', journalist Bronte McKnight's grandfather went missing in action like so many Allies, pushed to the southern beaches by the German invasion. During a holiday in Greece, Bronte is persuaded by her expat father Angus to finally help solve this family mystery and find out what became of Kieran in southern Greece. The book is also a wonderful, uplifting love story with an ending you'll never forget.

How Greek Is Your Love? continues the story of journalist Bronte McKnight and her love affair with charismatic doctor Leonidas Papachristou. As Bronte tries to live and love like a Greek, she faces an unlikely predator in the village and must solve the mystery of a disappearing expat, a famous writer/actress whom she has been tasked with interviewing. The search will take her into deepest Mani, helped by her maverick father Angus and an unforgettable rescue dog called Zeffy.

Can Bronte in the end find a foothold in Greece or is she just a stranger in paradise?

Praise for A Saint For The Summer

"I absolutely love this book. The writing is spectacular." Linda Fagioli Katsiotas, author.

"Her memorable stories include genuine characters. I'm sad to say goodbye to them." Maria Karamitsos, author.

"Spectacular descriptions, snippets of history, a love affair and an intriguing storyline makes this an exciting novel." Amazon reviewer.

"Immerse yourself in Greek life and culture expressed in prose that is at times exquisite. I hope there will be more novels to come." Alan Hill, journalist/reviewer

Praise for How Greek Is Your Love?

"A captivating, entertaining and skilfully crafted book." Peter Kerr, best-selling author.

"Yet another brilliant book. Highly recommended." Richard Clark, author.

"A perfect title. A fast-paced story that is exciting and thought provoking." Pamela Jane Rogers, author.

"An entertaining read with lots of laughs, suspense and moments of sadness, so a few tears were shed." Sandra McKenna, Top 500 Amazon reviewer.

If you've enjoyed Marjory's books, please consider leaving a review on Amazon. It will be very much appreciated.

The author loves making contact with readers either via her website (where you can also find books information and author interviews): www.bigfatgreekodyssey.com
Or on social media:

Twitter: www.twitter.com/@fatgreekodyssey
Facebook: www.facebook.com/MarjoryMcGinnAuthor
Instagram: www.instagram.com/marjorywrites

Printed in Great Britain
by Amazon

42216288R00136